'. . . And round it hath cast, like a mantle, the sea.'
ROBERT GRANT

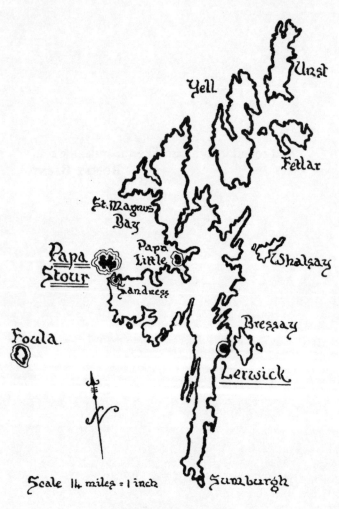

SHETLAND

Like a Mantle, the Sea

by STELLA SHEPHERD

Illustrated by
DENNIS H. SHEPHERD

THE SHETLAND TIMES LTD
LERWICK

First published 1971 by G. Bell and Sons Ltd.
First published by The Shetland Times Ltd., Lerwick, 1985.
This edition 1999.

ISBN 1-898852-51-0

British Library Cataloguing-in-Publication Data
A catalogue record for this book is available from the British Library.

Front cover photograph: Aisha Stack, Papa Stour.
© Paul Turner.

Printed and published by
The Shetland Times Ltd.,
Prince Alfred Street,
Lerwick, Shetland ZE1 0EP, UK.

FOREWORD

This book is not intended to be a geographical survey of Papa Stour, nor yet a detailed history of the island. Rather is it a means of putting on record the events of eight years, and depicting a way of life that, to me, seems both rare and refreshing.

My thanks are due to George P. S. Peterson for his help and advice, to T. A. Robertson for permission to include his poem, 'Da Sang o' da Papa Men', and most of all, to the islesfolk who made this book possible.

S.S.

CONTENTS

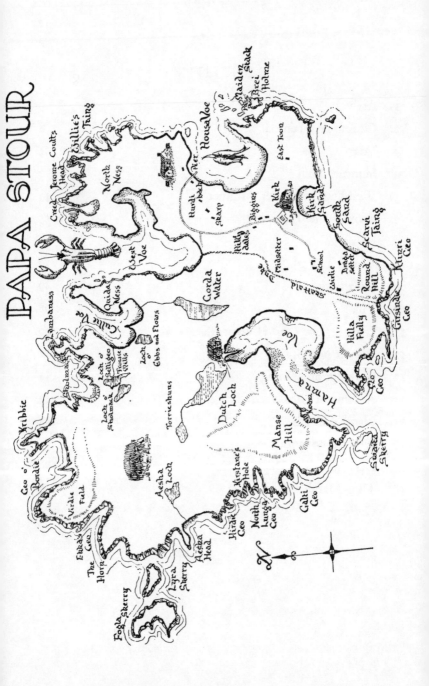

PAPA STOUR

Maiden Stack
Brei Holmæ
Creeva Crooks Head
Willie's Taing
North Ness
HousaVoe
East Toon
Hurdi back Kirk
Kirk
Sharp
Kirk Sand
Biggins
West Voe
Sooth Sand
Housa sand
Midsetter
Scarvi Taing
Gorda Water
Quadas Ness
Culla Voe
School
Wirlie
Dalgod setter
Housri Geo
Round Hill
Gruslnda Geo
Loch o'
Ebbs and Flows
Seahallo Dyke
Dumbaness
Hilla Field
Stolma
Hamna Voe
Loch o'
Loch o'
Stolma
Salligeo
Funzie
Cruis
Virda Geo
Bordie
Torrieshuns
Dutch Loch
Co
Geo
Loun
Vridie Field
Aesha Loch
Manse Hill
The Geo
Horn
Fraxs Geo
Swarta Skerry
Aesha Head
Hirdie Geo
Kirsham Hole
North
lunga Geo
Galti Geo
Lyra Skerry
Fogla Skerry

N

1 Arrival

THE CABIN ON the M.V. *St. Clair* seemed very full. Cluttered with cases and clothes, there seemed hardly room to turn. I lay in my bunk with its neatly tucked-in sheets, and knew that this cocoon state would soon be over. One way of life was being left behind, and, soon, a new one would begin. Lying in that pleasant twilit state between sleeping and waking, I became aware of a change of vibration. The deep throb of the engines had given way to a lighter one, and there being no motion on the vessel, I realised we had arrived in Shetland.

By easing myself up on my elbow and pulling the curtain aside, I could see across the tiny cabin and through the porthole. The picture I saw in its round frame was so beautiful as to take the breath away.

A pearly dawn light suffused everything. The sky, the puffs of clouds, the dappled water, even the gulls on the ship's rails had a quality of unmoving calm. This gave me the impression of looking into one of those glass toys children shake up and allow to settle. It was a glimpse of a new world—our new world. I marvelled at the difference that twelve hours could make. For, so short a time ago, and from this same porthole, I had watched the dockside hurly-burly of Matthew's Quay in Aberdeen as our furniture container was swung over the heads of the crowd and into the hold.

Now, in place of Aberdeen's drab wharf and its oily flotsam, there was the clean freshness of a Northern morning and the grey houses of Lerwick etched sharply against the sky.

But Lerwick was not our ultimate destination, just an entrepôt. For my husband and I were on our way to Papa Stour, one of the smaller isles lying on the western side of the mainland of Shetland. We were going to take up the joint posts of missionary and teacher there. The day ahead of us was to be a very busy one. A good many urgent things had to be attended to, and many necessary business calls to be made, including a visit to the removal agent, to the coal merchant and the bank. As we had had no previous experience of island life, we took local advice to cover every foreseeable contingency, and among many other things got ourselves fitted out in rainwear and rubber boots for the final stage of our journey which was to be in a small open boat.

But between us and that boat lay an overland journey of twenty-eight miles, and as there was no public transport, it was necessary to hire a car. During the day our luggage had snowballed and it spoke volumes for the springs of the car that we and our belongings travelled so well.

The road to Sandness, our point of embarkation, was fascinating and full of interest. Single track for much of the way, with passing places, it curved and twisted, now following a long inlet from the sea, then crossing a narrow arm of land, passing dun-coloured peat banks or skirting silvery lochans, now climbing over one fold of hills only to reveal further folds of muted grey beyond.

Now and again the car had to slow down while sheep hesitated and then crossed the road in search of scanty grazing. Although it was early May, the earth had not yet taken on spring green, except in a few sheltered places. The windward slope of the hills looked scoured and bare; a group of small ponies standing close together by a stone dyke, their manes and tails blowing, emphasised the laggard seasons in these northern latitudes.

Rounding the shoulder of a hill, the driver of the car slowed down yet again, but this time it was not for vagrant sheep, but to draw our attention to the first sight of Papa Stour. It lay there, with its lovely softly-rounded low hills, about two miles offshore, separated from the mainland of Shetland by a stretch of blue water, deceptively calm . . . Papa Sound.

Rattling over a cattle-grid, past the scattered houses, the shop and the post-office, we literally reached the end of the road, a rather dilapidated small jetty. Out of the car and on to the pier the luggage came and was piled up in an orderly way. The driver was paid, the car returned along the road to Lerwick, and we were left standing there. Northwards across St. Magnus Bay and beyond it, to Ronas Hill, our eyes followed the play of light and shadow on the mainland cliffs, warm-looking in the westering sun.

A small object on the sea, which kept disappearing and then reappearing in a slightly different position, grew almost imperceptibly until it became the size of a nutshell, and then could at last be identified as a boat. My husband was all excitement and, jumping up from his suitcase seat said, 'Well, here it comes at last! So we are not forgotten after all.' 'That can't be our boat— not one that size,' I replied, with some misgiving. But I was mistaken. The boat drew steadily nearer to land, the engine was shut off and the little craft slid up alongside, bumping gently on the old motor tyres slung along the jetty.

A cheerful face, creased and tanned by the weather, beamed up at us from beneath an old tweed cap. 'You're the new folk?' a cheery voice asked, and with handshakes all round, he introduced himself as 'Lowery'. With amazing agility he heaved himself out of the boat and on to the pier, and immediately began lowering our many cases in. It was only then I noticed what a low ebb there was, and I realised with sudden clarity and some consternation that the sea would play a major role in our new life, and I had a good deal to learn about it.

I noticed that the luggage, of irregular size and weight, was being stowed with seaman-like consideration for the boat's trim, and I wondered why such particular care was being taken for what appeared to me to be such a calm crossing. Indeed I had a lot to learn. The very next moment I had to learn how to embark grace-fully and retain a certain degree of dignity, not an easy thing in town clothes overlaid with waterproofs, and from a slippery weed-covered pier into a rocking boat.

All safely aboard, Lowery cast off, and as the boat drifted away from the pier and I saw the gap widening, I had a sudden feeling of finality. The last link with all familiar things was severed.

I was suddenly recalled from my reverie by the alarming rock-ing of the boat as Lowery cranked the reluctant engine. After several attempts his efforts were rewarded with a splutter and a bang, and we chugged along happily.

As we left the lee of the mainland, we began to feel the lift of the great Atlantic swell. About midway the engine coughed and stopped. A momentary panic filled me as I saw the land disappear from view as we sank into the deep troughs, and reappear again as we rose on the next swell. I knew now, why, to us standing on the jetty a little earlier, the boat had appeared and disappeared. Now the positions were reversed. The boot was on the other foot.

Lowery, unperturbed, clambered over the cases, removed the engine cover, unscrewed the sparking plug without the aid of a spanner, scraped it with a rusty knife blade and put it back, finger tight! Then he inspected an old cocoa-tin covering the petrol tank filler cap, started the engine, and we proceeded upon our way.

After this interesting episode we began to look about us more, and borne in upon me was the truth of the Breton fisherman's prayer, 'Protect me O Lord—my boat is so small and Your sea is so great'. For here we were, three tiny human beings, a speck, no more, in a blue immensity of sea.

As we drew nearer the island, I began to soak in the sights and sounds and smells. The isle was fresh and beautiful, green and redolent of that island smell with which we were to become so familiar, an aroma compounded of freshly turned earth, the salty tang of seaweed and the occasional drift of wood-smoke. And the boatman told us that the smell would be even better in the summer when the clover bloomed, and that, in the past, fishermen far out at sea, could find their way back to the island in darkness or in fog by the scent of it.

I could see two small sandy beaches separated by an outcrop of rock. I could pick out houses, school, crofts and kirk. Sea-birds were everywhere with their raucous cries and plaintive calls. But I think the smells delighted me most that day.

Lowery also explained that rather than take us to the pier, which was at the northern end of the island, he intended to land us on the more southerly of the two beaches I had seen, because of the quantity of luggage we had. This beach, though convenient for the schoolhouse, presented difficulties in landing, he added, because of what he called a 'run'. This was a swell with a very strong undertow.

The boat's stem was run up the beach; Lowery leapt overboard, standing in his thigh boots in the small breakers, keeping the boat steady, while case after case was manhandled by a small reception committee of two on the beach, one youth and one young lady.

Then came the process of getting ourselves ashore. Waiting for the strategic moment between 'runs', my husband jumped over the bows and landed on the sand. I had the choice of a jump or a pick-a-back. Not wishing to give a ludicrous first impression, I opted for the high-jump. Work roughened hands helped me up on to the gunnel. I waited for the word from Lowery, and at a shout, I jumped. Two size-three footprints were impressed alongside two size-nines. We were here! We had made it!

The immediate task was to get the luggage above high-water mark, and this we did in Red Indian portage manner. This was imperative, and when we could pause to take breath, the youth was already disappearing over the hill. The young lady introducing herself as Mary, shyly pointed out the schoolhouse to us, and I could see that between it and us lay two uphill struggles and a hollow of boggy land in between. The day was getting warmer. Town clothes are not ideal wear for such a task and by the time the last boxes and bags were off the beach we were extremely hot. Then alternately stumbling over stones and sinking in the wet boggy ground, we made our way towards the house.

Then it was that I saw the best sight of the day—a fine grey curling plume of smoke rising from the schoolhouse chimney.

There are some houses with which one falls in love at first sight; they have appeal and charm. But this was not one of them. Built on to the school, it appeared square and boxy, plain and of 'no-nonsense' style. Solidly built of island stone and roofed with slates (a fact we had cause to rue later), it had a small unfinished, unroofed extension sprouting out of the north end. This was to be the new kitchen.

If the outside was plain, the inside was bewildering, with its thirteen doors on the ground floor, each of which was a potential entry for draughts. Looking round the premises, both upstairs and down, made us poignantly aware of our predecessors, transitory tenants; hooks where a child's swing had been fixed, a reminder of happy hours; paint scored by pramwheels as some harassed mother coped with a stiff door on a windy day; faded marks, the ghosts of long-removed pictures, on wallpaper; a nursery frieze; little things to make us wonder who had been here before us, what they were like and where they were now.

But time for reflection was short. The tour of the house had shown that there were no amenities whatsoever, no light, no water, no sanitation. It seemed that life for a short time, at least, was going to be a glorious Girl-Guide safari, and none of the romantic notions of 'a lone shieling on a misty island'. Although known officially as the schoolhouse, it had been used some time previously by a temporary nurse, and the authorities concerned had provided a modicum of furniture and utensils which had not yet been removed.

While I was dusting and arranging these things and my husband was unpacking a few necessities, there was a knock on the door. Mary, who had previously helped us in our disembarking, stood there smiling, offering me eggs, and some milk in an undisguised whisky bottle.

The milk suggested refreshment to us. But first we had to find a kettle—the nurse's. Then we needed water, and a bucket to carry it in from the well. As Mary helped us with these chores, she shyly admitted that it was she who had been in previously and lit the fire.

A little later, as all three were sitting round the hearth on improvised box-furniture, my husband remarked that he had never tasted such good tea, adding, 'It must be the milk.' Mary and I exchanged covert smiles as our eyes met over the whisky bottle, and this has been a source of amusement to us ever since. The afternoon was sliding gently into evening, and as the morrow was Sunday, Mary suggested that it might be a wise thing to visit the shop—the island's one shop—for food and other immediate necessities. It was, she said, at the north end of the island, and she gave us very comprehensive directions to enable us to find it; along the track, past the kirk, through a small wooden gate, up a grassy hill and over a stile. We got there all right, but found that it was much more than a shop. As well as being a post-office, it was a meeting-place where island news and views could be exchanged, and Alex, the shopman, a mine of information. The shop had that nostalgic smell which is the very essence of all general stores, a blend of cheese, apples, bacon, paraffin and Stockholm tar, laced with the mealy smell of old sacks. And while Alex scooped up sugar and weighed it, sealing and patting the bag, and sliced bacon in the old style with a long knife, or measured tether-ropes in fathoms between his outstretched arms, he also dispensed humour and advice with kindly interest.

My husband and I, standing just inside the double storm-doors, were drawn into the general conversation, and later, when the other customers had gone, Alex, as an Elder of the kirk, gave us helpful advice and details of the Sunday services.

It had been planned, he said, that the minister of the parish—the parish of Walls—of which our island was a very small part, would come to take the morning service and introduce my husband as the new missionary, or minister's assistant, to the congregation. But this, of course, like everything else, depended upon the weather. If the wind freshened and Papa Sound became rough, no boat would be able to get across.

Back home we settled down to write a sermon and a children's address, in case the minister was prevented from coming. Time was short, so I helped by looking up quotations and checking Bible references, balancing my pile of books on a suitcase, while my husband wrote rapidly, his writing-pad on his drawn-up knees. Both of us realised that to arrive on a Saturday was not the best of arrangements. But an evening's close co-operation had the service complete and ready. Turning our attention to domestic affairs, as our own furniture was not due to arrive until Monday (tide and weather permitting) it was necessary to investigate the mysteries of the nurse's put-you-up bed-settee. This turned out to be more of a let-you-down, as the manufacturers, with fiendish cunning and an uncanny knowledge of anatomy, had placed a supporting bar where it would play havoc with the pelvic girdle, and protruding springs to prod the small of the back.

As soon as the rectangle of window took on the grey of dawn, we quit the 'joke-bed' and Sunday had begun.

Our fears about the weather were unfounded. The minister came, as planned, and after the service we shook hands with the islanders we had not hitherto met. It had delighted us to see families together in the pews, and I had a chance to get a preview of the scholars I would be teaching the next day.

The fine weather continued on into Monday, and while filling my pail at the well I paused, looking eastward to the main-land, where even the details of the houses could be clearly discerned. The clarity of light and needlesharp visibility augured well for the arrival of the *Margaret Shearer*, the converted fishing-boat which was due to bring our furniture that day.

Breathing deeply the chilly but invigorating air, straight from the sea, I thought how lucky I was to have left behind the smoky city. But ironically enough, as I opened the school door, I found the schoolroom full of smoke. From then on, the whole tempo of the day changed.

Coping with a smoking stove was just one of the many unexpected things to be tackled in that first crowded day.

Back in the house, when school was over, I washed in the nurse's small bowl, but I might have done as well in her eye-bath. After an evening stroll, which had the twofold purpose of covering ground for a future nature walk, and giving me time to reflect on the day's events, I returned to do battle with the 'joke-bed'.

But sleep was a long time coming that night. The impressions of the day, so many and so varied, drifted like an untended flock of sheep.

The sun had set, but there was still the rosy flush of its afterglow that tinged the clouds with coral and pink. I lay there a long time looking at the sky, until my thoughts, like the day, faded into grey infinities.

2 Getting Acquainted

THERE IS AN old Shetland proverb which says, 'A silk Monday makes a canvas week', implying that if a Monday is fine enough to warrant the use of silken sails, the rest of the week is likely to require the more rugged canvas variety. So fine Mondays are quite often looked upon with a certain amount of misgiving and distrust. In this particular case, however, the fine day suited us well, for while I had been busy teaching in the school, my husband had been down to the pier when the *Margaret Shearer*, with our belongings aboard, tied up. When I was told about the unloading of the furniture afterwards, and heard of the struggle the men had had, I regretted that I had not been able to leave the school and witness this feat for myself. The task must have been herculean, manhandling a ton of coal and all the heavy goods ashore without the aid of a crane, and then heaving them into a trailer behind the island's one tractor. Johnny, who owned the tractor, made six trips that day, from the pier to the house and back, each a distance of about one mile, joggling along the stony, uneven track. It was to his everlasting credit that the only damage in all that transshipment and removal was one broken tumbler and the knob of the butter-dish. Surely that must be a record for safe driving.

The nurse's furniture was removed, and ours took its place. Our beds were erected and crates were unpacked. With our own things about us we began the process of settling in. And although we still stubbed our toes on the unfamiliar stairs, barked our shins on unexpected corners and longed for a miner's helmet in the dark recesses, the house began to take on a more familiar look.

An orgy of scrubbing entailed constant visits to the well, but now there was neither temptation nor time to stand and stare. The weather pattern had completely changed, bearing out the truth of the old proverb. The subsequent days were canvas ones all right. Rain-laden winds from the west began to blow, and raging with a suddenness we had never experienced before, lashed the water out of the pails we carried. So we arrived back at the house, with only half a pailful for our efforts, and soaked from the knees downwards into the bargain. Nor could we escape the wind and the rain indoors. That wind found every chink, whistled through every ill-fitting door and undulated the carpet. It lifted the slates on the roof in a curious way and then dropped them again, so that the sound effect indoors was like that of someone pushing a wheelbarrow overhead. Instead of the orthodox windows, the bedrooms were fitted with small skylights. When the sun was shining, we woke feeling like lettuces under a cloche, but when the rain began, we were hard put to, to find vessels enough to catch the drips. A heavy downpour would produce a steady drumming, while a spasmodic shower gave an effect similar to that of the ancient oriental water torture.

The weather of the remainder of that week not only fulfilled the proverb, but gave us a startling insight into its vagaries. The heavy salt spray, blown right across the island, seared the leaves of some young plants and bushes we had brought with us for the school garden, until they looked as if they had been scorched by a blow-lamp. The spray caked the west-facing window-panes with a salty grey deposit, rendering them semi-opaque.

But the weather had still one more trick in store. One afternoon that week, as I eulogised to the children about traditional May Day festivities in England, waxing eloquent on maypoles and sprigged muslins, I noticed that all their eyes were turned window-wards, where snow was flying past horizontally and a little settling in the corners of the panes. Snow in May!

It was about that time, during those early days here, that the Sinclairs, a family on the island, had been planning to go over to the mainland to attend their daughter's wedding. Two of my pupils, George and Edwin, brothers of the bride, were all agog to be present at the ceremony. But, despite all the preparations, the weather had the last word and prevented them from crossing Papa Sound. That storm, and the snow, and the way people accepted it philosophically made us realise that learning to live with the weather was of paramount importance if one was to retain any serenity of mind.

In those early days we deceived ourselves into thinking that the thick stone wall surrounding the school ground would afford some degree of protection from the onslaught of the weather. But we were soon disillusioned. The wall created a sort of aerial whirlpool, in which things could be funnelled upwards. It was comic to see this happen to someone else's hat, but almost unbelievable to watch a large enamel wash-bowl take off in a similar way. It was one thing to chase to the next croft for errant tea-towels from the washing-line, but it was quite a different matter when a woollen blanket fringe was unravelled and wound round and round the boys' toilet building.

But within the school walls, many changes were taking place. It was a scene of great activity as the workmen dug trenches for the sewage pipes. The school garden had somewhat of the aspect of a 1916 battlefield, an illusion increased by small, spasmodic explosions and little puffs of earth and stones, as gelignite was used to blast through the larger rocks, the soil being only a few inches deep. The school-bairns enjoyed every minute of it, making exaggerated gestures every time there was a bang. It amused the grown-ups too, some of those living at the north end of the island asking us the next time we were in the shop if we had declared war or were after Home Rule for Papa Stour.

It was a time of great activity, and it was patently clear from the earliest days of our life here, that the expression 'Do it Yourself' was a way of life and not merely a sales gimmick. I am of the firm belief that a missionary must be a handyman as well as a holy one, and I have been glad on many occasions that my husband has an aptitude for practical things.

A few days after our arrival, Helen, the wife of our immediate neighbour to the north, came with a strange request. The third finger on her left hand was swollen and sore, and she asked my husband to cut off her wedding-ring. When this was successfully and painlessly completed, there was general amusement in the thought that the 'Church' was responsible for putting the ring on, but seldom, if ever, asked to remove one. Scarce half an hour had passed when Martha, our neighbour on the south side, asked for urgent attention to her wireless-set. Situations, we have found, often arise, where a little practical help is far more valuable than a lengthy and learned discourse from the pulpit, practical problems of everyday living that can't be solved by theorising.

One of the funniest situations that arises on this island centres round the problem of hair-cutting. It happens that my husband is possessed of a very healthy head of hair, wiry and very thick. But it also has a great disadvantage; it grows phenomenally fast. Before we came here I took the precaution of buying clippers and a hairdresser's kit, and it seems to me that I have a regular weekly job, for no sooner have I trimmed his locks than he is back again, asking for a 'short back and sides'. From this small beginning my clientele grew, and so, through practical matters, and in the course of our respective work we began to get to know the islanders; and we were no longer regarded as 'unken bodies' (strangers). At that time, however, some of the menfolk were away in the Antarctic with the whaling fleet, and their return from South Georgia coincided with the end of the school term. At the school prize-giving ceremony, which everyone on the island attended, I tried, under cover of what was called on the programme 'Teacher's remarks', to run my eye over the assembled gathering and pair off man and wife. Although there were only about fifty people on the island then, this was a more difficult task than would be supposed, as, to my undiscerning eye, many of them looked alike. And this was not surprising, since most of them were related to each other, and many had the same surname. To complicate matters further, even the surname was not always used, but to differentiate between those bearing the same Christian names, the house name was used. Thus we had Willie o' East Toon, Willie o' Bragasetter, John o' da Haa' and John o' Midsetter; Mary o' Wirlie and Mary o' Biggins: and where a child was named after his elders, he became merely Peerie (little) Willie or Peerie John.

But I learnt a lot more on that Prize Day than just names. Afterwards, in conversation, I realised that despite being geographically remote, the people amongst whom we now lived were by no means out on a limb; I savoured their vital awareness and their appreciation of the important things of life. I learnt, too, that the element of surprise and freshness is a very valuable thing in island living.

Ceremonies being over, I closed the school door, and my husband and I set off for a walk. This was really the first opportunity to have a good look at the island from the summit of the hill behind the house. So, crossing the open rising ground, Da Murrens, behind the school, we made for the gate (called in Shetland, a grind) past a well and up the stony shoulder of the hill to the bad weather watch hut at the top. What a sight we had! The island, roughly three miles by two, was laid out below us like a map. A stone dyke cut the island in two from north to south. The west side, uninhabited and rather larger, was bare and brown, stony, like a lunar landscape, relieved here and there by small patches of green. The eastern part, where all the houses are, looked more hospitable and was greening up in the sunshine. The crofts, separated by wire fences, their ploughed rigs dark with rich earth, made a patchwork effect like a quilt. The white-washed houses each with barn, byre and 'lambie-hoose' looked like toys at that distance. Here and there the sun caught the shine of a newly tarred roof and glinted on a skylight.

Westwards our eyes roamed over the browns and russets that rolled towards the western cliffs, and over the many hollows filled with tiny, silvery lochans (locally called shuns).

Immediately below us was Hamna Voe, a large almost landlocked inlet from the sea, lying so still that it looked like beaten copper. In one magnificent sweep we could encompass the mainland from Watsness in the south, Huxter with its frill of white foam, past Sandness and across the wide expanse of St. Magnus Bay to the Eshaness lighthouse in the far northern distance. Westward, the sea, the open Atlantic, and down to the south-west, the island of Foula; and all around us a profound sense of space and peace. The sea, looked upon by so many with apprehension or as a barrier, we found ourselves regarding as a protective and enfolding mantle.

3 Voar

ROUGH SEAS AND turbulent weather are not usually looked upon with much favour by most people. But the equinoctial gales, though fierce, do serve a useful purpose here. The heavy seas and gigantic breakers, exceptionally strong in March and September, bring with them large quantities of seaweed.

Papa Stour with its deeply indented coastline of approximately twenty miles has several large bays, or voes, and many narrow steep-sided inlets called geos. All of these get their share of seaweed. Along some of the beaches it is scattered haphazard among the rocks and boulders; on others it is strewn in a regular curving arc, a deep thick bank of it, brown and glistening in the pale sun. This is one of the rich harvests of the sea, and from time immemorial it has been gathered in baskets, carried up to the arable land and used as fertiliser for certain crops.

One bleak cold day in March, I caught sight of two figures labouring up from Rivera Sands on the south-east side of the isle, just below the croft of Bragasetter. Each was carrying a heavy load, and as they drew nearer, the figures resolved themselves into the persons of Mary o' Wirlie and Frances, her future sister-in-law. Both carried kishies heavily laden with seaweed.

The kishie, a type of home-made basket, is shaped rather like an inverted bell. It sits comfortably upon the back and is supported by a rope which passes round the upper part of the chest. As there are no trees and bushes indigenous to the island, the original kishies were made of dried docken stalks, woven together very firmly, and were masterpieces of craftsmanship.

While Mary and Frances were making their many journeys from shore to croft, I pictured others doing the very same work. It was the right state of the tide, and I visualised Jessie, John o' Midsetter's wife, and Helen down by the tide line at South Sands, Katie Drummond and her daughter Muriel working their way steadily along the piled-up bank of seaweed on Kirk Sands, with Mary o' Biggins and her sister Lizzie doing the same, all filling their kishies with the seaweed and carrying the precious loads of nature's own fertiliser up to their peerie yards.

One spring day a few weeks later, we offered to help at a croft where two extra pairs of willing hands were needed. The seaweed had already been mixed with stable manure, layer for layer, in a large heap, and it was our job to spread it on the land. My husband volunteered to barrow it from the pile to wherever it was required. I armed myself with a fork and began spreading. Because of the salty tang of the seaweed, the job was not so odorous as would be imagined. We were told, in fun, it would give us an appetite, and it really did.

The ploughing followed this operation, and the way it began put me in mind of Mrs. Beeton's cookery book. 'First catch your ponies.' The two ponies that were fetched from beyond the dyke and harnessed for work that day were Brookie and Lexie, and it was with a thrill that I saw the first furrow being turned.

For me it is always a magical moment as the first clod of earth is turned over. The cutting open of a new furrow fills me with an appreciation of a pioneer's love of opening new ground. Each spring, that moment never fails to awaken in me a feeling of expectation, the first step in the annual miracle of renewed life.

While this work had been going on upon the rig, an old sail had been spread out in front of the barn, and corn was being threshed with the hand-flail in the traditional island manner and in exactly the same way as in Bible days, the wind blowing the chaff away. But it was sharply significant that another wind, namely the wind of change, was blowing, for although the corn was sown broadcast in the ancient manner, the sower went forth with a modern plastic pail.

As we were all enjoying a welcome cup of tea when the work was done, someone happened to mention the very heavy seas round the island. We had heard the distant rumble from the west side, a deep steady roar like an express train, and as some little time had elapsed since we had been to that part of the island, my husband and I decided to take a walk.

The wind was as bitter as ever, and emerging from the shelter of the stone dyke, we felt its full blast. It had been blowing steadily for several days, and had stirred up the Atlantic, and we could see the repercussion. Huge rollers were coming in, and the light caught the acid green colour the moment before they broke in a smother of foam on each skerry and headland. Spray was being flung explosively up the face of the cliffs, falling back in white trails, only to be hurled upwards again, endlessly, ceaselessly pounding.

We stood on the cliff top, but not too near the edge, leaning into the wind, at a point called the South Horn. This was near the site of the old Horn of Papa, a curious rock formation shaped like the horn of a rhinoceros. It was seas such as we were watching now that swept it away in a great storm of 1953.

As we made our way southward along the cliff tops, we passed Stour Hund, Little Huns Geo and Burrigeo, pausing at the boulder-strewn beach of Aesha and sheltering behind the ruins of an old water mill to wipe the salt from my husband's glasses and camera lens. Lying just off-shore we could see two small steep-sided rocky islets, Fogla Skerry and Lyra Skerry, looking very ominous with the treacherous swirling current between them. Lyra Skerry is the nearer of the two, and undercut with a series of caves of its own, it resembles a gigantic table standing on the legs of a Colossus. It had cormorants and fulmars aplenty. On the perpendicular sides they, along with kittiwakes and gulls, can live and breed undisturbed, absolutely safe from human interference.

We had been told that, until fairly recently, crofters used to take sheep out to Fogla Skerry by boat. At one point on the rocks of the skerry it was possible for a landing to be effected, and the first man ashore climbed up by a rope secured to a ring fixed in the rocks. After him went the sheep that would be left there to graze on the high grassy slopes throughout the summer. A venture of this kind could only be undertaken in the best of weather, with no swell and no wind. Though this practice is now discontinued, we could see, as we stood there, the ring still fixed to the high rock, and the remnants of a decaying fence.

The flattish rocks of the Brinings, an outcrop at the southern end of Aesha beach, were a lather of white foam, and as we pressed on past Muckle Hurdie Geo and Bennie Geo we could hardly hear each other speak for the roar of the sea below us, booming in the sea caves in which the western coast of Papa Stour abounds.

At Kirstane's Hole we stood for a moment or two to watch the tumult of water as it thundered into the cave, wave upon mountainous wave. Of all Papa Stour's caves, Kirstane's Hole is perhaps the most interesting, for at some time part of the roof of the cave has collapsed leaving a massive natural arch, and then, continuing deeper inland, ends in darkness on a small subterranean beach. Passing in turn North Lunga Geo and Brei Geo we paused for breath at Galti Geo, all steep sided and awe-inspiring in this stormy setting. Looking backwards along the way we had come we could see an expanse of short salt-soaked turf, strewn with stones and pebbles that the sea had flung up. And from that viewpoint we could hardly see Fogla and Lyra Skerry for the flying wrack and mists of grey spindrift.

Turning inland, with our backs to the wind, we set our course for home. It was a pleasant relief to get into the lee of Manse Hill and skirt round the shores of Hamna Voe.

But the sea was still turbulent there, restless with an urgent flow, the waves beating upon Sander's Beach with tremendous force and impact, then retreating over the shingle with a noisy sucking ebb. Not five yards away from where the waves were breaking along the shore and spilling over the stones in cream and brown foam, we found violets. They grew, among the irregular rocks and broken boulders, where the grass finished and the shore began. Rich dark purple flowers, tender green leaves, delicate stems.

We crouched low out of the persistent wind to examine the little beauties, amazed that such delicacy and fragrance were possible in so fierce a habitat.

Yet they were perfect, and I was made poignantly aware of the sharp contrast between these lush living flowers and the dried one I had found only that very morning, pressed between the pages of a school Bible. I mused over the thought that maybe that was what was wrong with the churches of today—too many pressed violets, folk bound to their Bible all right, but spiritually confined in rigid sectarianism and outdated dogma, with all the sap and vigour long since dried right out of them.

*   *   *

With the gradual depopulation of the smaller islands like Papa Stour, it becomes more and more imperative, as manpower dwindles, to work together for the important jobs, and for the general weal. This is especially true in the case of work where much has to be done in a short time, like potato planting in the voar, or spring. In the old days of large families, when Papa Stour had no shortage of manpower and no problem of depopulation, the 'tattie rigs' were delled or dug by hand, three people working together using the Shetland spade. The whole back-breaking operation took about three weeks. This is obviously impossible now, and in recent years Johnny has acquired a double-furrow plough as an attachment to his tractor, and he is in great demand upon the various crofts to do the ploughing prior to potato planting.

On these occasions there is general bonhomie as the helpers gather together, each with a pailful of seed potatoes, ready to follow the plough. At intervals down the side of the rig stand sacks of seed ready for replenishing the pails, and working together as a team, a rhythm soon develops. And the job that used to take three weeks is now accomplished in a matter of hours.

At first we were the targets for some good-natured teasing as we helped at the potato planting. They didn't expect, they said, that our tatties would grow, as we were 'Sooth bodies and didnae ken'. But actually we did not notice any difference at harvest time. Swinging our empty pails as we walked from one completed rig to another awaiting planting, the conversation turned to the all-important topic of weather. In the golden evening light everything looked idyllic, the gentle contours of the Roond Hill, the deep Mediterranean blue of the Sound and the warm pink of the distant mainland cliffs, and nearer to us the clean grey and white of the seagulls as they settled on the newly turned earth. We waited a little while as a new load of potatoes was wheeled out in a barrow, and instead of idling the time away, looked about us at the sky and the clouds for indicative weather signs.

My husband, having recently acquired a boat of his own, was anxious to learn all he could about the vagaries of the weather and the variation of the tides. George, Mary's brother, knowledgeable about all facets of island life, kindly volunteered to give us detailed information about what he called 'medes'. This word could most nearly be translated as 'bearings'. He told us, for instance, the correct medes for avoiding 'baas' or under-water reefs, treacherous rocks and dangerous skerries; the best medes for a good crossing of Papa Sound to the mainland, good medes for safe landings at the beach below the schoolhouse, and, most generous of all, good medes for fishing for ling and haddock.

The tides were also explained, not only by George that evening of the voar planting, but by many of the island menfolk during the course of the next few weeks. They were all anxious that no error of judgment should be made, and each in his own particular way voiced the warning that with Papa Sound there is no second chance. George came round to see us one evening some days later, making time somehow in all the busy round of the voar work, to give us a full account of all the tides, spring tides, flood and stream. He had taken great trouble to write all this down, and we could tell by the meticulous details he had listed, and by the gravity of his voice when he explained the complexity of the tides in Papa Sound and the problems they create in embarking, setting a course and landing, that the sea was not a thing to be regarded lightly.

Perhaps the hardest work in the whole busy round of the

crofter's year comes at lambing time. The weather, always an adversary to be watched closely, seems to do its worst in May, when the lambs are arriving. A tardy spring with little grass, makes it hard for the ewes, and prolonged rain, cold winds and sometimes sleet and snow combine to make conditions which are not at all propitious into which the lambs are to be born. Like humans, so often perverse, the lambs frequently choose to be born in the middle of the night, or in the early hours of the morning. Black-backed gulls and crows, taking up strategic positions on the gable end of a derelict croft house, a fence post or a byre roof, watch for an opportune moment and swoop upon the defenceless new-born lambs, pecking out tongue and eyes with savagery and cruel waste. These enemies necessitate constant human vigil, so during this time the crofter is somewhat of a stranger to his bed.

The weakling lambs have to be carried home, tended in any handy cardboard box, usually a biscuit carton, placed by the side of the stove, fed on warm milk, and the weak little spark of life encouraged by gentle rubbing. Though this is a pitiful sight, more tragic is the death of a ewe. The familiar calendar picture of a lamb being fed from a bottle often covers a sad loss.

We occasionally see another side of lambing, a comic one—the sight of young lambs wearing an old discarded Fair Isle sweater, wrapped up for warmth against the bitter winds. The jumpers are back to where they started. The wool has come full circle.

A somewhat unusual feature of the sheep rearing as practised here is the tethering of ewes. A familiar sight on any spring evening is that of a crofter-wife, Jessie, Helen, Mary or Lizzie, leading on a rope, a ewe, with a lamb or maybe twin lambs, following after, as she takes them to a new piece of grazing. If she happens to be at some distance, one can see her stoop to hammer the tether peg into the ground with any handy piece of rock, and after an appreciable pause hear the sound of the hammering.

This sound and the sound of the arrival of our migrant terns are sure signs that spring is really here. They seem to bring with them a lightening of everyone's heart, and people tell each other eagerly, 'They're back, the tirricks have come again.'

With spring fever in our blood, I took the first opportunity of a fine day to go with the children on what is now called in school jargon, 'environmental studies'. We were bound for the remains of the Leper Colony.

No one living on the isle now can remember with any certainty of detail who exactly the lepers were, or where, on the mainland, they came from. It is generally assumed that the leprosy from which they suffered was not the tropical form of the disease, but more probably a deficiency condition affecting the skin and due to insufficient or inadequate vitamin content in the food. With little or no medical attention, the disorder would spread, and no doubt be exacerbated by rough winds and salt-laden air. Tradition has it that they lived in an enclosure beyond the stone dyke in 'felly hooses' (rough dwellings made of turfs or fells) and that food was left for them on the dyke each day by any charitable person who could spare a little from their own meagre store.

We came to the Leper's Well first. The ground round it was temptingly green, but with that characteristic lumpy look of mossy ground that can be as full of water as a sponge. So climbing higher to avoid getting our feet wet, we rounded the shoulder of the hill, and came down upon the remains of the Leper's dwellings by a gentle gradient. Here, where the poor unfortunates had spent their last miserable days, outcast and forgotten, till death merci-fully released them, the aspect was bare and inhospitable. The stony terrain and sparse grass seemed most uninviting. Nothing much remained but what appears to be the foundation layer of stones to give any indication of the original size of the dwellings. It is said by the islanders that when the lepers died the turf roofs fell inwards and the huts were allowed to fall, or were pushed in, and so burial was as simple and unceremonious as that.

The children climbed about the moss-grown stones and found, inside the enclosure, a drift of white violets, so thick that it lay like snow. As they gathered bunches of the little flowers to take home, and I gazed enraptured at the fresh sweet beauty covering up the ancient scars, I pondered over the thought of the swift passage of time, in which Man and his works could so soon be forgotten and the manner Nature has of turning so melancholy a thing into beauty so moving.

31

4 Summer Idyll

IT IS VERY difficult, almost impossible, to say just exactly when a summer day on Papa Stour begins. In these northern latitudes, in June, there is virtually no darkness at all. When at first people told us that it was possible to read a newspaper out of doors at midnight, we found it hard to believe, but we proved by experience that this was perfectly true. Without putting too fine a navigational point on it, the sun sets in the north-north-west, dips for a while below the horizon, to rise again in the north-north-east. At midnight all the colours of the flowers, the grass and the earth are clearly discernible, the sky is never quite dark and the clamour of the birds ceases only for about an hour. This long summer day may seem unusual for man, yet the rest of nature seems to adjust itself very easily.

Our usual alarm clock is Jessie's cock, crowing from Midsetter, a clear and unmistakable clarion for us to be up and doing. However, in the height of the summer, we are very often awakened by the sound of a gull landing on the skylight and plodding across it with its broad pink webs. One summer, our waking signal on many mornings was more of a tattoo, beaten upon the kitchen window by a crow pecking out the putty that held the glass in place. This curious phenomenon, startling in the extreme, puzzled us for a while. We could see no reason why the putty of that particular window should be any more delectable than any other, until we realised that the kitchen window is the only one facing north in the whole island. We surmised that, as it reflected the early morning light, the crow must have been dazzled by its glitter and been tempted to breakfast upon it.

But it does not seem to matter how early we rise there is always somebody up and about before us. Smoke from a chimney, or a figure on the skyline, imply that the nickname for Papa Stour folk, 'Papa scoaries', is well chosen. The word 'scoarie' is the local name for a young gull, and surely these must be amongst those early birds that catch the proverbial worm.

Already some of the menfolk will be out walking along the shores and headlands, looking for driftwood, the familiar white cap of Willie Drummond bobbing along by Hamna Voe towards Combe (Koam), or the purposeful stride of Jimmy Bruce en route for one of his many driftwood caches. Some of the womenfolk will be out early too, searching for the odd lamb whose birth is overdue, or moving the ewes to tether them yet again on new grazing.

Suddenly all the houses seem to come alive. Smoke spirals up from lums into the clear morning air. Doors open as women emerge to feed the hens. Kye are led out of the byres after the early morning milking. The sudden resurgence of life seems to affect everything. Calves on their tether-rope jerk and pull, kick and charge about. Lambs are everywhere, running and jumping off all four legs at once as if for very joy. With the sounds of voices carrying on the air come the distant clatter of a dropped pail, the sound of someone chopping wood, dogs barking, and high above all these domestic sounds, the clear jubilant trilling of a lark, rising to meet the new day.

The isle, like Prospero's, is 'full of noises, sounds and sweet airs that give delight and hurt not'.

To the uninitiated, long summer days on a beautiful island conjure up visions of blue skies and calm seas, with golden beaches to be lounged upon, and over all, an air of idleness and mañana.

In June, as a rule, we do have blue skies, calm seas and golden beaches, but there is certainly no lounging, no idleness and no mañana.

Mary o' Wirlie, in her capacity as school cleaner, arrives first, as regular as clockwork, to light the school stove, and to set the schoolroom to rights. I see her as she hurries down Da Murrens and disappears round the corner of the school wall. Then comes the familiar click of the school gate, and as I go to the shed for wood, we exchange greetings. Later when her work is done and I hear the clatter of pails, she explains that today she is going to be very busy, for in addition to her usual chores, she will be at the 'rooing', so I do not detain her. With a 'cheerio' she is on her way, striding back to the Wirlie.

On returning to the house, I find my husband preparing for work too, reaching for his concordance and setting his loose-leaf papers in order. Contrary to the popular belief that a parson has a one-day working week, he methodically sets aside each morning for study and sermon-writing. The typewriter is already on his desk, his Bible open, and as I leave to go to the school I can hear the tap-tapping begin.

My journey to school is really only a matter of coming out of one back door and going into the next, but on fine summer mornings it is pleasurable to lengthen this and to walk round the school ground. Looking eastward over the Sound of Papa, seeing the dancing sunlight on the water, the occasional flash of light reflected from a car windscreen on the Sandness Road, the cleanness and brilliance of the summer morning, makes me decide, as I stand at the gate waiting for the pupils to arrive, to choose 'All things bright and beautiful' to start the day. Gordon comes in sight first, walking cross-country wise, from Midsetter, swinging himself and his schoolbag over the two wire fences. Then the other children come, up the rising ground from where the track ends.

As I usher the children into school, I see, out of the tail of my eye, lines of washing beginning to blossom in the distance, that which is farthest away having almost the appearance of a line of white breakers against the blue sea.

While my morning's routine goes on in school, much as any

other school morning, lesson following lesson, through the open school door drifts the occasional far-off barking of the dogs as they round up the sheep for the rooing. The pure bred Shetland sheep have very fine wool, and this is not clipped off with shears. Instead, it is pulled off with the fingers. This is not a painful business, although it may sound so. Much of the wool is already loose, and the sheep would cast that particular coat in any case. The rooing is the pulling or removal of this wool, and it is usually a communal event. Helen, Peter, Katie, Willie and Jessie all work together. After the sheep have been rounded up, the crofters usually sit down upon the grass, the men with a sheep between their knees, the women with the sheep alongside them, and they begin to pull gently, easing off the wool and putting it into waiting sacks.

The sheep, freed from the weight of the fleece, emerge with the next growth of soft short new wool already visible, beautifully white and clean. And as Katie and Helen turn them loose, Jessie opens the hurdle to let in a new lot of shaggy sheep. Everyone wipes their hands, shining with the natural oil of the wool, and the work begins all over again. During the hot still day, the wool sacks fill up, and the colours—black, grey, natural, white and moorit—are sorted out and put into separate sacks.

Meanwhile, John o' Midsetter has walked over to the Post Office and collected the island's bag of out-going mail. Shouldering the bag, he walks the mile to the pier, meeting Johnny about halfway. On reaching the pier they row out in a small dinghy to where the bigger boat is lying moored off in Housa Voe. Together they get aboard, stowing the bag safely where no spray can drench it, for even on a fine June day they know how choppy the Sound can be at certain states of the tide, and always take every precaution for the safe and dry conveyance of the mailbag. After tying up at the little weed-covered jetty at Sandness, they walk to the Sandness Post Office, a distance of about a mile, and collecting Papa Stour's incoming mail set off again making the return trip.

The sight of the mail-boat returning is a signal for Mary O' Biggins (or Peerie Mary as she is frequently called). She, as the official mail-deliverer, sets off from home, walks to our Post

Office, where the mail will be sorted, and begins her round-the-island walk, taking letters, packets and parcels to almost every crofthouse. Her first port of call is usually the schoolhouse, and as well as letters, she brings us other news—the whereabouts of an eiderduck's nest and the arrival of a red-throated diver, the former near the loch of Selligeo, and the latter by the shores of Gorda Water, both freshwater lochs. She knows that this will be a matter of great interest to us and the children in the school, and with that she is away, the mailbag over her shoulder, to the next house, the Wirlie.

As my eye follows her receding figure, I catch sight of another, even smaller. This one is on the roof of the Wirlie Hoose, brush in hand and it is Geordie taking advantage of the fine summer weather to do his annual roof tarring. I can see by the glint of the sun on the shiny surface that his job is more than half done. A few minutes later, looking through the kitchen window in the opposite direction, I see the same scene with a different actor, and farther off still, at upper Biggins, Jimmy Bruce, at the same job, is on his roof, also plying the tar brush.

During the dinner hour, conversation turns upon the delights of the summer weather and the desirability of making the most of it. And I decide to rearrange my afternoon lessons and organise a nature walk.

The teaching of nature study, which I always enjoy, is greatly enhanced by the marvellous variety of wild life here. To avoid desultory wandering, I like to cover the ground myself prior to the actual walk, and each walk I organise has for its basis one special topic, though of course I do not close my eyes and ears to the unexpected bird or unusual natural phenomenon we may encounter. On a bleak day, for instance, I arrange a nature walk to study the stones and how they are weathered by water and by ice, and the children find numbers of examples of split stones and smooth rounded pebbles, searching for samples of erosion, returning to school with pockets bulging, weighing, as they say, 'stones heavier'. Another day we may stand with arms outstretched by an old stone dyke, and within that span we examine everything we find there—insect life, lichens and moss. On a delightful summer day we may take four clothes pegs and a length of string, and mark out a square yard of meadow, choosing the place at random for a flower count, marvelling at the ways plants struggle for the light. To vary the bird-study and avoid an annual lesson on birds' nests, as so often appears in school curricula, I take the children to a good nesting ground near Kirstane's Hole, and let them pace out a space for themselves, say fifty paces by twenty, and make a nest count, noting the species of bird, the number of eggs and the nesting materials used. Sometimes, as may be supposed, the results are not always what we expect. For example, a place which was remarkable one year for its numbers of terns, may have an increase of common-gulls and a disproportionate rise in black-backed gulls.

Each year the children keep full nature diaries, noting the date of the first daisies, violets and scillas, and recording the first arrivals of the migrant birds. And all of them, and the grown-ups too, are keen to tell us of the first tern or the first Voar Maa.

So deciding to take advantage of Mary o' Biggins' bird news, we set off to see the eiderduck and the red-throated diver, so that we can note the date and the place in our diaries for reference the next year, and the next, and the next.

But sometimes on nature walks, the results are unpredictable. The unexpected happens. Starting off in search of mosses, we catch a startlingly beautiful glimpse of a heron, standing motionless on long slender legs in the water at the edge of a voe, one bird standing erect, and its perfect counterpart inverted in reflected stillness beneath. Or sometimes as we stop by a stone crüb, a wren pours forth its sweet sharp notes in a sudden burst of song, before flicking its tail in its own characteristic way and darting off to a hole in the stony causeway.

The most unexpected find we ever had on a nature walk occurred one warm June day when we set off looking for flowers. The island was already carpeted with flowers, and we had watched during the preceding days the vista towards East Toon change from just the green of grass to the green-and-white of a daisy covered slope to the green-and-yellow of buttercups. The discussion had taken the form of 'flowers on the windward side of the island have very short stems', and bearing this in mind, we left the schoolroom and books behind and set off. Across the Murrens, through the grind in the stone dyke we went, and did not begin our search till we were well over Manse Hill. We found thyme and sea pinks, and roaming separately and then coming together again to compare our specimens, we measured the length of their stems. In the bright June sunshine the turf was brilliant, smooth, green and finer than any lawn in a cultivated garden. The clumps of thrift and thyme dotted prodigally about were not only studied but genuinely admired. Then we walked schoolwards, finding milkwort, blue and pink and white, then butterworts, deep purple in their green stars, and then tormentil. And each was duly noted down and comments made upon the shortness of the stems.

But when we were almost home, Gordon, one of the pupils, found the exception. It was a buttercup the like of which I had never seen before. It stood there higher than he was, with a stem as thick as my thumb. The boys gathered round and gazed at it in wonderment. This monster disproved all our theories. It was obviously not in the pattern. The oddity of it made everyone look round about for any other signs of freak growth, and within a very small area we found several daisies with curious oval centres and stems that looked as if several had been fused together into one.

Back at school we examined these finds more closely. The daisy stalk was as thick as celery, and as grooved. The buttercup in its jar needed support, so flaccid was its stem. There were plenty of questions from the children. Why? Why? Why? About that time I had heard that on the market there was a weed-killer that was selective, and killed by simply making the weed outgrow itself. This was the only solution I could offer as explanation, and the boys volunteered the idea that, as no one on the island used that sort of thing, perhaps a migrant bird had brought some on its beak or feet, and the flowers we had found had been affected by it.

When the children had arranged their other treasures on the nature table and gone home, I propped up the buttercup again, and reflected that here, before me, there might be a modern parable. After all, feeding a flower on noxious chemicals till it grew out of all proportion, had no real strength, became flaccid and needed propping up, might quite easily be applied to some of the younger generation, who, not only physically bigger, have also been puffed up by false beliefs, fed on doubtful theories until they are swollen with self-conceit, hollow-hearted and need bolstering up in time of crisis. But perhaps I judge them too harshly. Still, it was a point to ponder as I closed the school door and went home to make tea.

Over tea, my husband and I exchanged the experiences of the afternoon. For my part, I had been concerned with the wild life of the island, and naturally my conversation turned on flowers, birds and their nests, whereas his turned on people and their works.

In the course of his afternoon he had seen evidences of great industry. Jimmy Bruce was mowing the churchyard grass with the scythe, carefully cutting round the uneven headstones, awry with time, and avoiding the clumps of red campions that grow there and add a bright dash of colour against the grey stones and walls.

Further along the road, leaning over a fence, my husband had spoken with Muriel Drummond who was energetically scraping their small flat-bottomed boat, prior to repainting it. In the lee of the house, in a sheltered sunny corner, her grandmother, Papa Stour's oldest inhabitant, sat on a chair enjoying the warm sunshine. But she was not idle either. She was busy knitting one of her specialities, a Shetland shawl, fine, delicate and lacy, with its rows of four hundred and eighty stitches each in their intricate pattern.

Two or three hundred yards from this scene of industry, another man was hard at work, Alex Scott, busy hoeing his potato rigs, waging the endless war against weeds, which flourish prodigiously in the short growing season. He was so busy and obviously had so much more work to do that my husband did not stop to talk, but passed on, with a wave and a shouted greeting.

On his return journey, he caught sight of Jimmy Jamieson busy, like Muriel Drummond had been, refurbishing his boat, but he was working nearer the shore, at the southern end of Housa Voe, at a place called the Mellings.

And when my husband was almost home, and had reached the point where the track ends and the ground begins to rise, just below the school, he stopped to have a word with our nearest neighbour, Myra, who was starting the mammoth task of gutting the previous evening's catch of fish, and then hanging them up to dry.

All this activity—everyone busily making the most of the long daylight hours—emphasised the fallacy of the popular idea that life on an island in the summer is an Arcadia of idleness and ease. Nothing could be wider of the mark. Even the 'exiles' home for holidays get busy, the men making lobster creels, repairing fences and gates, and white-washing, while the women start hoeing and hay-making.

But teatime was by no means the end of the day's activities. I knew that while I was in my kitchen men and women throughout the isle would be hoeing the weeds in the potato rigs, all busy about their crofts while I prepared food for the John's Mass 'banket'.

This is an old island tradition. On June 24th which is John's Mass, it is customary to hold a picnic or banket (banquet) at midnight and to watch the sun go down. Usually the children and young folk meet about 11 p.m. and walk to a suitable point at the northern end of the island, a headland or promontory offering unobstructed views of the late sunset and early sunrise.

So my evening was a busy one, preparing food, cutting sandwiches and filling flasks. Hardly had the last flask been corked when the school gate clanged, and the children, eagerly anticipating the adventure, trooped in. When our destination had been discussed and fixed upon, bearing in mind the direction of the prevailing night breeze, we set off with bags and baskets.

On the outward journey the children chattered excitedly, eager to show my husband the nests of the eiderduck and the red-throated diver that Mary had discovered and told us about, eager to share their enjoyment of nature with him. Passing the ruined remains of one of the many small water mills we made our way

along the shores of Cullivoe, an inlet from the sea. We selected our
banket place with particular care, and the site we chose had all the
requisite 'conveniences': lots of flat stones to sit upon, a larger
stone, more or less even, to use as a table, and all sheltered from
the night breeze, but, most important of all, giving an uninter-
rupted view over the sea to the northward. And just in the same
way as Robert Louis Stevenson rejoiced in his perfect alfresco
bedroom among the pines of the Cevennes, we revelled in our
perfect natural dining-room among the rocks of Cullivoe.

The banket had all the fun and enjoyment usually associated
with a picnic, but with the added excitement of watching the
light in the northern sky as the sun dipped lower. The boys busied
themselves by collecting small pieces of driftwood and breaking
them where necessary by the simple expedient of dropping a
heavy stone on them. Then, using the unwanted food wrappers,
they soon had a fire burning.

As the light faded and midnight approached, we gathered
round our stone table and began the traditional feast. We slowly
became aware of faint breathings other than our own, gentle
splashing and a soft susurration. We knew we were not alone.
Our company had grown. In the pale pearly light, the water of
the voe shimmered under the breeze, and here and there the
surface was broken into widening silver rings, ripples made by the
heads of our visitors, the seals.

Although it was midnight and the sun was actually below the
horizon, it was by no means dark. The world still had colour.
Rusty brown seaweed below our feet, orange lichen on the rocks
above us, clumps of thrift, a wash of pale pink. It was all there,
muted.

Muted, too, were the sounds of nature. The birds were silent. A
pre-dawn hush had fallen on our world. I had a momentary feeling that this might have been the Dawn of Time. Water, rocks
and things primeval waiting for the coming of Light.

Subtly, imperceptibly, I sensed a change, as if a pulse quickened.
The pale mauve smudge that had been the mainland hills took
on substance and the water of St. Magnus Bay became faintly
luminous. This one hour of Simmer Dim seemed little more than

a brief pause, a breathing space, when nature shook off the day's heat, not in the heavy darkness of sleep, but like infant slumbers, pure and light.

I was not alone in sensing this change of rhythm, this quickening towards the dawn resurrection. The birds, silent for an hour, suddenly, as if released from bonds of silence, burst forth in their dawn chorus. A new day had begun. Behind the distant hills, now darkening to purplish-blue, a band of gold spread across the sky and flooded the wakening waters, and the sun catching a wisp of cloud, flecked it with gold and gilded its edges.

As the light broadened and everything seemed to be reborn, the children, in a fresh burst of vigour, stamped out the embers and packed the picnic things and we began our homeward journey. With many a backward glance, to observe how the sun was climbing the sky, we walked on, and I noticed that, as is often the habit of children after excitement, they grew reflective and reminiscent.

In this mood we were passing Gorda Water when one small bright speck, no bigger than a bead dropped on the ground, caught my eye. Like a light, it winked and vanished. We all stopped and found in a hollow clivmet (a pony's hoof mark) a small brown Richardson skua chick. It was perfection of camouflage. Only the winking of its bright beady eye had given it away. But for that slightest of movements, we would have passed it, unnoticing.

So, just as it is difficult to say when a summer's day on Papa Stour really begins, it is equally difficult to say when the day ends.

A drift of blue scillas in every corrie, the wafted scent of clover and thyme, and all threaded through with day-long lark song, blending the sights and sounds and scents into the very essence of summer, till yesterday becomes blurred into today, and today becomes tomorrow's vignette.

5 Weddings and Later Summer

As THE YEAR matures and each long sunny day brings a sense of fullness, I for one at any rate feel like John Keats' bees, that warm days will never cease. And this, in me, is coupled with a sense of wanting to cling on to summer as long as possible, of seeing it stretch out, on and on, enjoying the beauty of the island, and being out of doors as much as I can, and for as long as I can.

One little task which I like to prolong during the summer, occurs every Saturday evening. It is the pleasant job of gathering flowers to decorate the communion table in the Kirk. Usually I set off with a basket, a pair of scissors and a plastic can of fresh water. I amble down the sloping ground in front of the school-house to the stretch of marshy land between it and South Sands. There, a blaze of marsh marigolds, juicy-stemmed with globes of gold, awaits my choice. I cut and snip, filling my basket, and as I glance round I can see no appreciable difference. I cannot tell that any flowers have been taken so great is their profusion. With a basketful of these and plenty of their dark green leaves for background, I make my way to the Kirk, where, in the tiny vestry, I fill the vases with water from my can, and arrange the flowers ready for the morrow.

Some Saturdays I gather red campions, or purple orchis.

Sometimes Muriel, another ardent flower-lover like myself, brings bluebells, huge perfect specimens. Sometimes there may be bunches of the red clover for which the isle is famous. As the summer progresses, the bunches vary, but always they are bonny and bright.

Tourists from England who once happened to be visiting the island, went to have a look inside the Kirk, and commented enthusiastically upon the wild flowers there. They told me with pride of the ornate floral arrangements in their churches, and, somewhat wryly, of the petty vying that went on among the donors, anxious to outdo each other's efforts, and incidentally missing the whole point of taking flowers to decorate a church. But there is nothing like that here. Putting wild flowers in the Kirk seems like giving the Lord His own again.

It was after such an expedition on a Saturday evening in the summer, when dawdling along in the mellow gold, that I had a lovely find. I had really completed my work, gathered the flowers (marsh marigolds on that occasion), been to the Kirk, and was on my way home, leisurely swinging my empty plastic can. I had just passed Barnie Houlls, a piece of rising sandy ground, honeycombed with rabbit burrows and, on that evening, carpeted with flowers. I glanced down at my shoes, seeing them lightly powdered with yellow pollen dust, and as I looked, I noticed a bird fly up suddenly from the grass at my feet. My interest being aroused, I stopped to investigate and there, hidden away by the long grass blades, was a lark's nest. A small tightly woven home about the size and shape of a teacup. How cleverly hidden the nest was, and cleverly hidden, too, by colour were the three tiny eggs. How hidden was the enormous promise contained within the three fragile shells. How hidden the wings that would one day take the bird spiralling upward. How hidden the tiny throat and the song that would, next year perhaps, fill the blue spaces of another summer sky.

Watching a nest from day to day gave me a wonderful excuse, if any excuse were needed, to go out of doors and linger while the delightful weather lasted.

The schoolchildren discovered a bird's nest under the irregular stones of the island 'road'. Each time they passed it, or I visited the place, we noticed fresh things about—wisps of straw, feathers, grass and shreds of sheep's wool—until one day our vigilance was rewarded with a glimpse of the owner-occupier, a starling, flying in with a grub in its beak. The unusual position of this nest, and a unique hole for peeping into, afforded many excursions and accounted for plenty of enjoyable loitering, as did the arrival of the Snowy Owl.

This ornithological news set all the telephone wires on the island buzzing. A visitor to the island reported to have seen the Snowy Owl first. Then a Papa Stour man, Bruce, home on holiday, positively identified it. Then there was no holding me back. Off I went to the place he had described. Along the narrow footpath leading to Virdiefield, the island's highest hill, I walked, leaving the track only when I reached the rising ground known as Hundsetts. Stony terrain, this, with plenty of cover. I walked up the uneven slope looking assiduously all round as I went for any glimpse or any sign of the bird. When I reached the summit of the tiny coll, the grassier place known as the Skord of Hundsetts, I paused for breath, and there, in the boulder-strewn ground on my right, was the bird I sought, not fifteen yards away from me and in the act of flexing and unflexing its wings. It rose and flew off, strongly, majestically, yet not in any hasty wing-beat of alarm, and came to rest about thirty yards away, erect, and again flexing and unflexing its wings. The glimpse delighted me. I was tempted to follow for an even closer look, but decided against it, so as not to give an illusion of pursuit. It was generally believed that this bird was an offspring of the famous pair which nested upon the island of Fetlar on the east side of Shetland.

But as the summer advances, life is not entirely composed of bird-watching and flower gathering. Indeed, sometimes when I lazily watch a bee pressing down upon the clover flowers in search of pollen, or I gaze skywards following the mazy flight of the circling terns, I remind myself that other people are hard at work, and remember the old fable of the ant and the grasshopper.

Pleasant though it is to see the summer dervish dance of gnats and to watch the myriad small insects skim the surface tension of some lochan, I cannot idle away the summer time. I bestir myself to collect up the library books which are housed in the school, and arrange for next year's supply to be sent from Lerwick. A mammoth task this, and when the last book has been checked and the last screw tightened on the heavy wooden boxes, my husband takes them in his wheelbarrow to a convenient point, where Johnny can transport them in his tractor and trailer to the pier, when John o' Midsetter will take them across the Sound to Sandness, as and when the weather permits. Then, by the reverse process, but by the same team-work, the new books arrive. Three heavy wooden boxes are deposited at the school, and there follows the pleasurable task of opening them and arranging the books on the shelves. With vicarious pleasure I sort out the juvenile books for the children, and with anticipation, the non-fiction, travel and biography from the 'who-done-its'.

Another mammoth and communal task in the summer is the transporting of coal. As there is no peat on the island, fuel has always been Papa Stour's number one problem. Years ago there was a poor quality kind of turf dug out on the west side of the island. But it had little or no heat-giving property and was most unsatisfactory in use.

The people had, however, peat-cutting rights on the island of Papa Little, an uninhabited islet some distance off. The obtaining of this fuel presented many difficulties, for in those days the boats were propelled by oars or sail. In fact it was not until after the Second World War that the first boat-engine came to Papa Stour. So, a peat-cutting enterprise was determined by wind and weather, and the availability of some able-bodied men to row. It might happen that, in the absence of a breeze, it was necessary to row there, a distance of approximately nine miles. And such is the swift changeability of the weather that just as the peat-cutting began, a sudden wind would spring up, making it imperative to have a rapid change of plan and without delay make a hasty journey back, watching the rising sea. In addition to these difficulties, peat is a bulky cargo, and when finally the peats were 'cured' and ready to be transported home, a year's supply for one household would entail many excursions between Papa Little and Papa Stour.

Now with the decline in the population and the decrease in manpower, this means of getting fuel is not only out-moded, but impossible. So now each summer there is 'operation Coal'. During the first June of our stay here, my husband and I tried to 'work' our own coal and the effort well-nigh killed us. We ordered the coal, three tons of it, from the merchant in Lerwick and it was duly delivered to Sandness in hundredweight bags. Choosing a calm day, we went across the Sound with two willing helpers, Willie o' Bragasetter and Victor, Mary's young cousin, who was here on holiday. Using our own boat, with a carrying capacity of only half a ton, we made six trips. Each trip followed the same pattern.

We crossed the Sound, tied up at Sandness pier, and while the two men barrowed the bags of coal down the narrow weed-slippery jetty, Victor and I held the boat steady. Recrossing the Sound, we unloaded at South Sands. Here, with no pier, the business of unloading was no easy one. While one of us stood in the water, steadying the boat, the other heaved a hundredweight bag on to the waiting shoulders, and the bearer staggered up the beach. Keeping the boat steady was a tricky job, remembering what Lowery had told us so long before about the 'run' of the waves on the beach, and bearing in mind the difference that one man's weight and a bag of coal could make to the boat's trim.

Then the coal was still only part of the way home. Salt water and weather rotting the fibre of the bags, till they split in one's grasp, did not help to make the job lighter. The sands at South Sands are of a particularly soft and yielding nature, making walking difficult. The moving of the coal from this point to the house was similar to the Red Indian style portage of our luggage the day we arrived, only much dirtier. Sweat and spray and coal dust had turned us into four giant pandas.

Since that experience, things have altered. John o' Midsetter, understanding the overall difficulties of island transport, was enterprising enough to buy a big boat, about twenty-five feet long, with a beam of nine feet six inches and a powerful diesel engine, also a good load-carrying capacity. This vessel, the *Venture*, has revolutionised our fuel and transport difficulties and is our main and vital link with the mainland. There are countless occasions when this big boat can cross the Sound, when it would be impossible for the smaller boats to do so. This is a tremendous boon to the island, as there is no public ferry and the transport is based on the island and runs from the island to the mainland and not, as might be supposed, from the mainland to the island.

But all the transport across the Sound is not so serious and laborious as coal-heaving. Sometimes it has been light-hearted, and on occasions, hilarious, as, for example, in the case of weddings.

Now, a strange situation obtains here regarding the solemnisation of marriages. The very small population of the island, and the fact that it is only a part of a parish (the parish of Walls), only merits the appointment of a lay-missionary, not a fully ordained minister. And a lay-missionary is not empowered by the Church of Scotland to conduct weddings. This raises two alternatives. Either the parish minister may be invited to come over to perform the ceremony, or the bridal party can go across to the mainland church to be married there. And the five weddings that have taken place since we arrived here have all been conducted on the mainland. Each, because of the geography of the island and the vagaries of wind and weather, has been a masterpiece of planning and organisation.

The first island wedding we attended was Patsy's. Her father, Alex the shopman, invited us, and, most cordially, included our relatives who were up on holiday with us. He also paid us the great but undeserved compliment of asking us to sing a quartet at the service, during the signing of the register. Patsy had a particular fancy to be married in the little church at Sand on the mainland, the church where her parents had been married. This necessitated extensive and complicated transport arrangements. All the islanders who were able, wanted to attend the ceremony, and as John o' Midsetter had no big boat in those days, the numbers presented quite a problem. Some days prior to the wedding, tentative arrangements had been made with a fishing boat, the

Utilise, to call at Papa Stour and to pick up those who were going to the wedding, all twenty-seven of them, and land them at Sandness. The actual day of the wedding dawned grey, sombre and pouring with rain.

My husband, who is a stickler for punctuality and seems to prefer all excursions to be run with a military precision, was out before breakfast, on the west side of the island, looking for the boat which was due to come in with a couple of hours in hand. He returned very wet and with no news of the *Utilise*. A change of clothes and breakfast over, he was off again, looking for the boat through the grey rain-curtains that swept in from the Atlantic over the island, eventually returning soaked again, still with no sign of the boat. By eleven o'clock the position was becoming urgent. It was obvious that other arrangements would have to be made. The telephone wires began to hum, and the upshot of it all was that Alice, Johnny's sister, rang up a relative of hers on the mainland, who owned a van, to ask him to contact the owner of the *Ajax* at West Burrafirth, the nearest boat of any size. Such is the co-operation and friendly spirit of these folk that within a very short time the familiar masts and stay-sail of the *Ajax* could be seen coming through the mists and rain towards our pier.

In the meantime the news had gone round and people were beginning to converge upon the pier. As I closed the door, I knew I had left behind me a kitchen that resembled the drying room of a laundry, and as we splashed along the road, avoiding its many puddles, I thought what unlikely wedding guests we seemed in raincoats, rubber-boots and sou'westers. The tide was at a very low ebb, and this necessitated climbing down a slippery iron ladder set into the concrete side of the pier before we could get aboard. Once aboard, the problem was how to stow everybody in, for this being a normal working day for the *Ajax* there was a large quantity of lobster creels and fish boxes taking up much of the available space.

Now, Sandness Bay is shallow, and as we approached the very end of the jetty, that being in the deepest water available, there was a gentle bump, and the stem of the *Ajax* rose a few inches.

We were aground. To get out of this situation it was necessary to lighten the for'ard end of the boat, run the engine in reverse and try to pull off the rock. This manœuvre being at last successful, we made another careful approach and managed to get near enough to the pier for people to clamber ashore over the bows.

At the end of the road, a little bus, previously ordered, was waiting, and we climbed in thankfully, glad to be under a roof of any sort. Many of the company were so wet by now that to sit down was most uncomfortable, and people began peeling off wet coats. A few miles down the road we turned off down a by-road to reach the kirk at Sand. At frequent intervals it was necessary for the passenger nearest the door to alight to open the gates that barred our way. The joggling of the bus increased at each gate we passed, as the surface of the road deteriorated. Our progress became a series of crashing lurches, when it was almost impossible to remain on one's seat, and the creaking windows became tortured parallelograms.

The transformation that took place at the church was amazing. From a drenched group of oilskin clad travellers there emerged smart wedding guests. Gay hats were taken from their protective plastic bags. Rubber boots were replaced by 'stilettos'. In the brightness and joy of the wedding service all the discomforts were forgotten. For me, a good deal of the pleasure came from seeing two of my pupils, sisters of the bride, so obviously happy being bridesmaids.

I had been used to English wedding receptions, usually short, and always very formal. By contrast this reception was gay, cordial and lasted literally all the night. The wedding feast, the lively speeches, toasts and the telegrams of congratulation were followed by dancing of a most energetic sort. One eightsome reel followed another—the lancers, barn dances and the familiar Shetland reels—and while the band played on and the young folk changed partners again and again, their elders, sitting round the perimeter of the room, exchanged reminiscences of other weddings and bygone days with old friends.

And so the night passed, and as a grey dawn was breaking we found ourselves once more aboard the *Ajax*. A few Papa Stour people who had not crossed the Sound when we did but stayed on the island to attend to their animals, had followed later in their own boats. So now, a little flotilla set sail, bound for Papa Stour.

Perhaps the loveliest touch of all to the wedding occurred the following day when the bridal party visited each one of the 'auld anes' on the island, in order to show them their wedding bouquets.

There is an interesting and picturesque tradition connected with weddings on Papa Stour. In olden days it was the custom to have what was known as the 'Wedding Walk'. It was arranged after the wedding service was over that a procession, led by the fiddler, came out of the church, the bride and bridegroom first, followed by the bridesmaids arm in arm with the groomsmen, and then the guests in order of precedence. This whole long procession wended its way to every house on the island. In this way, old people who were unable to attend the ceremony saw the happy party in all their finery. There are one or two photographs of this tradition still extant on the island, and very treasured they are.

This charming custom was revived as far as was possible on the occasion of the wedding of George and Frances. It was arranged that the actual wedding service was in Lerwick, and because of the very wide circle of friends, a reception was held in Lerwick and another in Papa Stour. It was at this island celebration that the modern equivalent of the 'Wedding Walk' took place. After the wedding feast and the cutting of the cake, the toasts and the reading of the congratulatory telegrams, the bridal party went out into the brilliant sunshine, across the open ground to one croft-house after another; a colourful little procession to gladden the hearts of those who were housebound.

The dancing that followed was prefaced by the 'Bridal March', a very dignified and stately procedure, but as the evening wore on, the tempo quickened and the whirling rings of the eightsomes gave way to the straight sets of the 'Foula reel', which in their turn broke up into couples for the 'Gay Gordons'. And so it went on throughout the night, schottische following polka, the 'Dashing White Sergeant' after a breathless 'Strip the Willow'. And when the band paused for refreshment, George took up the fiddle himself, and never once repeating a tune, played on and on, 'Da Hen's

March ower da Midden', 'Da Four Poster Bed', 'The Mason's Apron', in rapid succession, and all with such a lively rhythm that even the non-dancers could not resist tapping a foot. In traditional fashion the merry-making went on until the morning, and looking at the windows, I saw the deep blue slowly pale and give way to the pearl and pink of a fine northern dawn. And as the sun rose fully up over the mainland hills, the wedding party broke up and people went their various ways wishing each other 'Good morning'.

In my mind these weddings have different and distinct associations, the one with the very wet day, and the other with its flavour of old island traditions. But the wedding of Lizzie and Billy conjures up thoughts of a different kind. They, like the others, were married on the mainland and held their reception on Papa Stour. It was in the darkest part of the year, when things are always at a low ebb. Winter seemed to have been long with us, and spring still afar. And into this gloomy doldrums came news of a wedding. The effect on everyone was amazing. A lightening of the heart, the joy of the forthcoming celebrations, and what was more cheering still, the knowledge that a new man was to come to live on the island. This sort of joy can only be appreciated by someone who lives in a small community. With so few people, and particularly so few men on the island, Lizzie's wedding and Billy's decision to settle here were the cause for much rejoicing.

That dark grey day the schoolroom, which is always the room used for such functions (there being no other accommodation available), was transformed. Gone was the atmosphere of school; of chalk, ink and exercise books there was no sign. In their place were long tables, bright with snowy cloths and shining cutlery, and flowers in vases on windows and tables turned the room into a bower. The gaiety and brightness of the wedding reception made everyone forget the murk of the night, and beneath this gaiety lay the comforting knowledge that in place of an empty house there would be another lighted window and another smoking lum.

The wedding of Johnny and Eileen took place while we were away on holiday, a situation we regretted but were unable to alter. Although we were very disappointed at being away from Shetland just then, the news of the wedding had about it the same overtones of rejoicing as had Lizzie's.

Both weddings had something in common. Both were bringing a new person to the island, in the case of Lizzie's a new young man, Billy, was coming to live among us, and in Johnny's case, he was bringing a new bride, Eileen.

In an island so small as Papa Stour, everyone matters, and the addition of one new person is tremendously important. It represents a new personality, a fresh face, and above all it means someone with new ideas and thoughts. And in these days when the general drift is away from the smaller islands and communities, when the pull of the cities is strong, it is all the more cause for rejoicing when a young couple decides to settle.

When the Drummond family announced the engagement of their daughter Wilma, the island had just passed through a very harrowing time. That winter had been particularly long and hard, and made much more difficult to bear because of the illness and death of two of the community. The news of the forthcoming marriage and all the plans to be made buoyed everyone up wonderfully. And I noticed with great poignancy how the islanders felt for each other, in the winter, sharing each other's sorrow, and then rejoicing in mutual happiness over the prospect of a wedding.

Looking back on the island's weddings, I often say that Wilma's and Donald's was the one we nearly missed. Returning from a holiday by plane, we were grounded in Orkney by fog, and spent a day and a night in Stromness, kicking our heels and wishing the weather would clear. And between listening to doleful weather reports, we wondered how the wedding plans were going. However, by about noon the next day, conditions were a little improved, the flight was resumed, and coming down through a keyhole in the clouds, we landed at Sumburgh, and got to the wedding in time after all.

True to tradition the reception had that Shetland blend of dignity, joy and cordiality. For after the wedding breakfast, there was enjoyment for young and old; merry-making, energetic dancing, lively music and easy good fellowship, the revelry lasting, undiminished, until morning.

But however late or 'early' the revelry of any wedding lasts, everybody knows that the routine croft work must go on. The animals must be attended to and someone has to milk the kye.

So on the 'morning after', life resumes its normal tenor. Chickens are fed, sheep are re-tethered in fresh grazing, and the feet that have lightly tapped the night away to the lively rhythms of the fiddle, now plod rather wearily between byre and rig.

The crescendo of excitement that culminated at the wedding, so expressive in the German 'hochzeit' or high-time, is over. There is a perceptible slackening in the tempo of life. And it does not seem to be confined to human life only. It is discernible in the whole of nature.

Subtle changes take place. One morning, when indoors everything seems damp and clammy, and bread sprouts a growth of bluish mould, out of doors the little pale gentians that grow near the site of last year's bonfire are becoming sere and brown, and in the dew-drenched grass this year's generation of starlings can hold their own against their elders in the unceasing quest for food, and against the stone dyke the reddening docken stalks stand laced with gossamer.

Some of the early migrant birds will be already gathering together prior to departure. And the old discarded nesting sites are quiet and deserted. It is then one realises that the turn of the year has arrived.

Though there still may be a few visitors on the island—relatives, married sons and daughters at some of the croft houses; though the school is still on holiday, there is a palpable difference.

Mornings misty and evenings cooler, and the sun's daily arc sliding slowly southwards.

6 Trokers and Transport

IN SOME OF the not-so-very-old Shetland archives, there are accounts recording the difficulties of transport. In the past, Church of Scotland Ministers in Shetland who had, of necessity at times, to travel to Edinburgh for ministerial meetings, found it more expedient to sail from Lerwick to Holland, and from there to take ship to Edinburgh. This seems to have been quite a common practice, there being a better sea-link between Lerwick and Holland than between Lerwick and Scotland in those days.

Things are not quite as bad as that now, but travelling still does present many difficulties. This is true particularly from the smaller islands, like Papa Stour. Most of these difficulties are 'natural' ones, that is difficulties which arise from natural phenomena like rocky coasts, treacherous submerged reefs and swift tides, which can only be safely negotiated by long experience and an intimate personal knowledge of the hazards.

For example, each approach to Papa Stour presents a different set of problems. To disembark at South Sands, a boatman must locate a submerged rock known as 'Da Bist' which lies awkwardly in the very path one would normally take from Sandness to the island. Then there is the 'Run' Lowery warned us of, always a tricky business, and if passengers are not young enough or sufficiently agile to jump, they have to be carried ashore on the boatman's back. There is also a very steeply shelving beach to contend with, and added to this, there is definitely no possibility of 'mooring off'. A boat must come in, discharge and leave again at once, and the beach is only accessible to a small boat, at that.

The next bay to the northward is Kirk Sands, a very fine looking beach and most inviting, with its broad sweeping curve, but it is absolutely useless for effecting a landing. This beach, by contrast to that at South Sands, is so gently sloping that any boat would ground long before dry land was reached.

The most commonly used landing place is Housa Voe, a large bay on the north-eastern side of the island. It is in this bay that the pier was built. But like all the other landing places on the island, it has disadvantages too. These lie mainly in the approach. Coming from Sandness, it is usually approached through a narrow rocky channel between stacks. This is called 'The Pass', and the position and angle of the rocks above the water are completely misleading. On the one hand is an outcrop of rock which appears gradually shelving above the water level, but below the surface it falls sheer away: while on the other side is a steep rock rising a little above the water, looking stark and forbidding, but, contrarywise, below the water this slopes off gently. And to complicate matters further this rock is submerged at high tide. The picture above the water is the complete opposite of that which lies below. A newcomer could be very easily fooled. To add to these complications, there is a diminishing line of stacks ending in a long underwater reef known as Stacka Baa. At certain states of wind and tide, this reef causes a great turbulence that results in a succession of breakers, which appear mountainous to anyone in a small boat. These breakers sweep right across the course of a boat emerging from the Pass into the Voe. It is very often necessary under these conditions for the boat to lie almost in the mouth of the Pass and wait for a lull in the procession of waves, which, to a newcomer, can be a nerve-racking experience.

With the boat engine in neutral, John o' Midsetter counts the huge breakers, waiting for the opportune moment, while the boat lies uneasily in a lather of white. As the lull comes, usually after every third wave, it is 'full ahead' and John steers into the calmer waters of the voe and heads towards the pier.

Hamna Voe, on the south-west side of the island, presents a very different picture. It is almost landlocked and affords good shelter, except from westerly gales, which make it impossible to enter or leave. Gales out in the Atlantic stir up very heavy seas on the western side of Papa Stour, and these break in bursts of white foam over Swarta Skerry (Black Skerry) which lies roughly across the mouth of the voe. The method of landing in Hamna Voe, or embarking there, depends upon the state of the tide. If the tide is full and there is plenty of water, it is possible to bring the boat up alongside an outcrop of rock known as Krogarry which forms a natural landing stage. If, however, the tide is at the ebb, travellers have to land or embark at a place called Da Kletts, where there is just sufficient water to float the boat. The rocks, slippery with sea-weed, demand careful movements, especially if people are carrying bags and suitcases.

I consider Papa Stour a most delectable island, with natural beauty and wild life second to none, with lovely bays and a network of picturesque sea-caves. Yet it could never be classed as a seaside place in the accepted sense of the term. I suppose its remoteness and its inaccessibility are responsible for this.

An incident occurred about two years ago when a lady, a native of Papa Stour living in Chicago, returned to the island for a holiday. She stayed with her brother, Willie o' East Toon, and when the time came for her return to the U.S.A., some of her Papa Stour relatives escorted her to the Sumburgh Airport at the southern tip of Shetland. Goodbyes were said and she flew south, to connect up with her trans-Atlantic flight, and the relatives set off back to their Papa Stour home. But such are the vagaries of weather and transport, that she had reached Chicago and put through a telephone call to let them know of her safe arrival before her escorts had arrived back on this island.

In spite of all the difficulties of transport and their attendant delays and discomforts, a few visitors come, and they are very refreshing. It is always good to see fresh faces, and they usually bring with them new ideas. They make a marvellous contribution to island life, invigorating it, enlivening it; for it is possible to become too insular. They are our window on the world.

Quite a number of people who come to the island for their summer holidays are relatives of the people here. Sons and daughters who have gone to Scotland, maybe for further education, married sons and daughters bringing with them their families, and natives of the isle who are now 'exiled' in the south all return to see the 'auld anes'. This is very cheery, not only for their immediate families, but for their contemporaries on the island, people who shared their childhood years. Being present at many of these happy reunions has given me a glimpse of what the island must have been like when it was more populous.

To hear middle-aged and elderly folk reminiscing over their Papa Stour childhood, when they carried their daily peat for the school fire, fished 'aff da craigs' (off the rocks), went away over to the west side of the island to catch their ponies which had been running free, and when they themselves ran about happy and barefoot in the sun, makes me aware that a way of life has vanished. As they wistfully recall these childhood scenes, setting them against the drab uniformity of multi-storey flats and the concrete monotony of modern city dwelling, I bring to mind those words of 'Auld Lang Syne':

> 'We twa ha'e paddled in the burn,
> Frae morning sun till dine'

and the lump I feel in my throat is for all the things that they have lost.

There is a more practical side of these family visitors, of course —namely, the extra pairs of hands they represent, forming a very necessary addition to the labour force on the croft. The men may be out in one of the small boats fishing, enjoying the sport, and very pleasant it looks too, as the sun sets over the voe, gilding the waters; but such is the way of things here, that pleasure can be combined with business. The fish will be taken home, gutted and salted down for consumption later. A walk along the seashore can be a thrilling recreation for children who have 'been long in city pent', and the driftwood collected can still provide a large part of next winter's kindling.

There are visitors who come here regularly, in an official capacity—for example, the parish minister, the doctor, the coast-guard, the vet and school inspectors.

I was vastly interested to hear an elderly lady on the island refer to such visitors as 'sitters'. And by way of explanation she said that in the early days of oars and sail (up to the Second World War) each Papa Stour man in the boat had to bend his back and pull at an oar. He was crew. But if the boat returned from the mainland, and watchers on the Papa Stour shore could see one upright figure, he was sure to be a visitor (probably some official) and was called a 'Sitter' to differentiate him from those who were rowing. There would, no doubt, be plenty of conjecture as to his identity. On one occasion our M.P. came, and his visit was recorded at the next island concert, in song, a verse of which ran:

> 'Ae day we wrought amang the hay,
> There cam a boat frae Sandness Bay,
> The 'sitter' he was plain to see,
> A certain very tall M.P.'

No name was needed.

But being a 'sitter' is not just as simple as it seems. A passenger may find himself wedged in between bags of nitro-chalk and hen-food, he may be 'sitting' on a box of over-ripe bait; his fellow travellers may be lobsters and crabs scratching about inside an old tea-chest, or he may be foot to foot with a ram, or find himself, as I did once, being watched curiously by the large long-lashed eyes of a calf. If the traveller is privileged to a calm crossing on a sunny day, he may find himself sharing a fish-box seat with the school medical officer or the G.P.O. telephone man; on a rough day he may duck for shelter against the flying spray, rubbing shoulders as he does so, with the coastguard or the vet.

The man under the next oilskin may be the optician coming for his periodic eye-testing session, or a school inspector, the Crofters' Commission man coming to measure fences, or it may be the parish minister. There is one thing that can always be said, the journey is never dull.

One occasion I remember vividly was when the schools' music organiser came across on an official visit to the school, as part of a series of studies he had planned with 'taped' lessons. On this particular day he brought a colleague along with him, connected with the Schools' Music Association. The weather was as bad as it could be, with heavy rain, and a wind so strong that the cruise ship *Meteor* could not land passengers on Papa Stour as had been planned. But the little boat got across all right to Sandness, and returning, deposited the two school visitors, dripping wet but undismayed, at the pier. They walked the mile or so, carrying between them a heavy tape-recorder, wrapped in a wind-whipped polythene bag, and an assortment of percussion instruments—cymbals, tambourine and so on—for the children's lesson. I was concerned for their general well-being. City clothes and city shoes are not designed for walking along a wet stony track in torrents of rain. By the time the morning session was over the rain had not abated, and I was even more concerned for their return trip which promised to be equally drenching. But my worries were unnecessary. By the next mail came a most enthusiastic letter full of the thrills of the crossing, describing it as the most exciting journey they had ever made. I have no doubt it was, for watching from the house, the boat kept disappearing from our view, beyond great waves and flying spray.

But there are, every summer, a number of visitors who come in no official capacity, but rather for pleasure or interest. And these are usually called by the island folk 'Trokers'. Some come for a few hours, others for a few days and some for a week or two. Occasionally the visitors who come for a few hours, for an afternoon maybe, expect a ferry service, saying casually that they may return on the next boat, or the one after, and seem rather nonplussed when they find there is no regular public ferry and the crossings depend to a large extent on the state of the sea. Very few people seem to appreciate that the question of travelling across the Sound by boat is very similar to making a journey by aircraft. When travelling by air, it is the take-off and landing that present the difficulties. The journey in between normally presents no problem. Similarly with the boat, it is the points of embarkation and of landing that are the doubtful factors. Normally the journey in between these two points, even in comparatively rough weather, does not present insurmountable difficulties.

Other trokers who come for a day enquire if there is an hotel on the island. Not a few ask for impossible things, and one, rather foolishly, demanded to know where was the taxi, the mobile ice-cream van, and where fish and chips could be bought. This, as one of the islanders so succinctly put it, was simply 'want o' wit'.

Some visitors, by arriving ill-prepared, become burdensome, as did a luckless youth who came with a tent, but had no water-proofs and no change of clothes. Others by pure misfortune, get stranded and receive harsh treatment by the weather. This happened to a party of three Crofters' Commission men. They came intending to remap part of the island, a thing which had not been done since the early nineteen hundreds. They arrived well prepared, with oilskins and rubber boots, but a fierce gale sprang up within hours, and the winds were so strong that it was impossible to use the theodolite, sighting stakes and measuring tapes. The tapes were snapped like thread, the stakes blew down, and the men, wet and wind-blown, had no option but to abandon work for that day.

Then came the accommodation problem. Two of them stayed with us in the schoolhouse. The following morning the weather was no better. The gale, far from abating, had increased, and weather-wise men on the island told us that once the wind had got into that particular airt, it might blow for a few days. It did. It blew for eight in fact, and each day the surveyors became more desperate to commence their work. Their situation was further exacerbated by the incorrect weather reports on the radio, and the necessity for these men to convey to their head office the reason for their long absence and to convince their superiors of the wildness of the elements.

Quite a number of summer visitors come with the express purpose of pursuing their hobby or following some particular interest. I remember a young couple interested in folk dancing who came with the intention of collecting information about the island dance 'The Papa Stour Sword Dance'. Another group of people came seeking some rare species of moths. Many want only a trip by boat among the fascinating network of sea-caves. Two visitors came asking if anyone on the island had any of the old-fashioned colley lamps to sell, as they were interested in collecting curios. One student came to gather information for a college thesis on the theme of 'life in a small community'. Others came to watch birds. Some, carrying cameras, are intent on photographing seals. Some come to camp.

A geologist came, and came again, collecting rock samples, complete with his hammer and his mapping materials, making a complete geological survey of the island. His enthusiasm for his subject and his unusual finds of exceptionally large agates, awakened in many of the island folk a new interest in the very foundations of their island home, and helped to give real meaning to the phrase 'sermons in stone'.

One summer we had a visitor of a completely different kind, Ella, a blind girl. It was with some misgiving on our part that the visit was arranged, as my husband and I realised that so many of the charms of Papa Stour are purely visual. We worried a good deal beforehand about the problem of her getting about, as the ground is rough, broken, and in parts boulder-strewn, there is no level and regular footpath, and the island 'road' is but a stony track. We need have had no qualms. Her sense of direction was particularly acute, so that she never got lost. She seemed to have a built-in radar. Her sense of touch and inborn caution helped her with safe footholds, and the feel of different types of ground beneath her feet—sand, gravel, grass or heather—seemed to give her a very good idea as to her whereabouts. Feeling the boat rocking on the Sound, and the steadier motion in the bay, gave her intense pleasure, and the sounds of little streams rushing and splashing, or the thunderous pounding of the waves beating against the cliff where we picnicked, seemed so real and vivid to her, that she was able to tell the islanders things she had noticed about Papa Stour which surprised them with their detail and accuracy.

Another interesting visitor who spent some time here was from the Museum of Antiquities in Edinburgh, and we thought, somewhat humorously, what scope he would have lodging with two old museum pieces like ourselves. Actually he was looking for discarded things of historic interest, agricultural and domestic, and he busied himself photographing old ruined houses and outbuildings, and examining water mills, old stone dykes and likely sites of ancient habitation. My interest quickened when he found 'knocking-stanes' for the grinding of corn by hand, a breast-harrow still used by Jimmy Bruce each spring, clibbers that Jessie o' Midsetter had used to put over the pony's back for carrying kishies full of peat. Like many of our visitors, he made a big contribution to the island life, stimulating its interest and widening its knowledge with a showing of film slides of parallel life in other islands and other small northern communities.

Perhaps the quaintest visitor we ever had, and one who came under his own power, was a lone Swedish sailor, Per Johan. He had sailed his little craft, *Pelle*, a twenty-two foot yacht of Bermudan rig, from his native Stockholm into Hamna Voe. But we knew nothing of this till he appeared at our back door with two empty plastic cans asking for fresh water and milk. Under his arm he carried a shopping-bag full of rolled-up maps and charts, and in broken English he introduced himself.

Over coffee he unrolled his maps and showed us, with some degree of pride, his course, adding that he intended to sail on to Faroe and Iceland. We carried his refilled cans back to the voe, and he ferried us in turn in his little soap-dish of a dinghy out to the *Pelle*. There we had the fun of being taught the rudiments of navigation by an expert, but in half-Swedish and half-English. He was a navigation enthusiast to the nth degree and took us piece by piece over all his radio-directional finding gear, and gave us a practical demonstration, getting a cross-bearing from Stavanger in Norway and Bushey Mills in Northern Ireland right on Hamna Voe, Papa Stour. There was an auxiliary outboard engine stowed in a locker, but it was evident that it was *infra dig* for a real sailor to use anything but sail.

However, perverse as the weather can be, for four or five days there was no wind at all—a flat calm, not so much as a breeze to flutter his pennant. Eventually, however, the weather pattern changed. A breeze stirred the waters. Per Johan appeared at the back door, his weather-beaten face creased into a leathery grin. Delighted at being able to set sail, he had come to say goodbye. He stood there, a jolly little fellow, straight from the pages of Tolkien, complete with his little gnome cap. My husband and I went to a point of land commanding a view of the entrance to the voe, so that we might see him sail out into the open sea. Then, Per Johan, blowing a small mouth fog-horn in farewell, sailed through the narrows. We watched his sail till it was a white speck in the waste of waters.

7 Hairst

IT SEEMS THAT boys the world over are attracted to water and enjoy fishing. Whether this is by a park lake, with a penny net and jam-jar, or less sophisticatedly by a stream with an improvised net made out of a discarded nylon stocking, it does not seem to matter. There must be lurking in every boy some of the old primeval urge of the hunter, to pit his skill and cunning, and his patience, against his prey.

And this is not confined to boys only. There is no age limit to this sort of thing. On any Saturday afternoon or Bank Holiday, by any river, canal or lake, in Britain, you can see the boys of yesterday still at it. Some may be knee deep, in high rubber waders, in the middle of a fast-flowing stream. Others may be sitting huddled under their large dripping umbrellas by a dismal grey canal, having set the keep-net hopefully at their side. Others may be in boats, flicking the waters of a Highland loch with a fly. Not a few of these will have elaborate and most expensive equipment, fine rods, an assortment of hooks, floats and flies, and most likely tins of bait, and in some cases, deerstalker hats and Norfolk jackets.

The purists would no doubt be amazed at the simplicity of the fishing equipment here, particularly that which is used in the form of fishing known as Da Eela.

Any reasonably fine evening in late summer or early autumn, a couple of Papa Stour men will arrange to meet just before sun-down. They go down to where one of the peerie boats is lying in its noost. This is a shallow excavation near the shore, the dug-out turf piled round to conform to the shape of the boat, to afford protection from the wind and gales and to stop the boat from being blown away. With scant conversation, for few words are needed between men of a practised team, they get on with the job of pulling the boat out and dragging it over wooden bars, called linns, towards the water's edge. Throwing in their gear, they climb aboard and push off, one man taking the oars while the other sits in the stern and prepares for action. The rowing is usually called 'aandowing', while the actual fishing, which will be done by his partner, is called 'draaing'.

The equipment is simple in the extreme. Two bamboo rods about ten feet long, each with a line of approximately their own length tied on, are got ready and held in place over the stern by the simple process of sitting on the inboard ends. Then, from under his tweed cap, the man about to fish pulls out a small coil of nylon to which are attached five hooks. Settling his cap back on his head, he attaches the nylon, with each of its hooks decorated with a small piece of white seagull feather, as a lure, to the line. He needs no bait.

By this time the little boat has reached one of the good places for fishing and the hooks are streamed out astern. The art of aandowing is to keep the boat just gently moving so that the hooks with their white feather lures are following along just below the surface. Row too slowly and the hooks sink; too quickly, and they rise to the surface. Once among the shoal, the man draaing has his work cut out to clear the hooks. As fast as he empties one line and throws it back, the next is tugging. The catch soon begins to cover the tilfers or floorboards of the boat, little shining sillicks, with tints of orange on their scales, pilticks darkly silver, both bass in the young stages. An occasional mackerel and a luya lie amongst them.

Then as the sun sinks and the voe becomes a shining shield of beaten copper, the little boat heads for the beach. Shipping the oars, stepping ashore, pulling the boat up, the two men still have the satisfying job of sharing their catch. Then slinging the büdies or home-made baskets on their backs, with the rope handle across their chests, each man makes for home.

This is the type of fishing known as Da Eela, and there are some phenomenal catches made. I was inclined to doubt my own ears when one of my pupils, a very small boy, told me his father and grandfather, fishing together in the same boat, had caught a hundred and eighty score. I privately wondered if the child knew what a score was, and tactfully said, 'Perhaps you mean a hundred and eighty altogether. That would be nine score.' But he stoutly reiterated his original statement of a hundred and eighty score. Just for interest I showed him how to work the sum on the black-board, and he was round eyed with wonder at the noughts. It was true enough, though, for later in the day, I saw his mother gutting them, all three thousand six hundred I suppose. She was sitting outside her house, fish boxes all round her, as I passed and she called to me that she had had an unusual find. 'It's a fish within a fish', she said, and it was obvious that the larger fish must have swallowed the smaller one immediately prior to being caught. It was indeed a curious sight, and I recollected that somewhere, years ago, I had seen a fossil of the same sort, a perfect fossil fish inside another fossil fish, hunter and hunted fixed for all time.

In the late summer or early autumn, just before the 'exiles' have to leave again, Papa Stour folk have an Eela competition. The method of fishing is exactly the same, two persons to a boat, and two rods with five hooks each. The fishing time is limited to one hour, the start and finish of which is signalled by the firing of a shotgun, usually by Willie o' East Toon, from some strategic position. The boys and men enjoy this immensely, choosing their favourite place to fish where they hope the catch will be heavy. George and his father push off from South Sands and fish about a hundred yards off-shore, while anyone looking across Housa Voe would be able to discern Alex Scott's boat, Jimmy Jamieson's, and farther off still, Muriel out with her father, while John o' Midsetter and Johnny Scott appear no bigger than specks out beyond Krugersetts. Meanwhile, other little boats are out in

Hamna Voe, some of the older schoolboys and one or two visitors, and when the final shot announces that time is up, the men and boys, with büdies, boxes and pails of fish come ashore to have their catches weighed.

If there has been a spell of rough weather, it can affect the fishing in two ways, churning up the feeding grounds and driving the seals close inshore for shelter, with the result that the competitors' catches are low. But if conditions are favourable, the spring-balance very often registers its maximum and still more pailfuls of the same catch stand waiting to be weighed. One year as Muriel's catch all but reached a hundredweight and I was congratulating her on a good result, she said, 'But wait till you see the others.' The winner that year had a catch of two hundred and seven pounds, all this in one hour.

After the Eela competition the women's work is to gut the fish and to salt them for use later on. Some fish may be used for baiting lobster pots, some may be boiled for supplementing the hen food. But some, I have no doubt, the very prime, will be eaten that evening for a tasty supper.

It never ceases to amaze me that this activity of fishing always follows after a very hard day's work on the land. Apart from all the daily routine chores of feeding the hens and milking the kye, there is the seasonal work, of which the most time-consuming is hay-making. Until recently the hay was cut by hand, with a scythe. If the weather is good, this can be a most pleasant job. And I remember a number of occasions, after the stuffiness and confines of the schoolroom, the refreshing sense of physical activity and freedom with which I wielded a hay rake in company with Helen. On a sunny day, in a hayfield, rake in hand, the turning of the swathes in an even rhythmic motion can be most satisfying, 'the tedding and the spreading' of the sweet-smelling grasses of summer.

But how different this is when the weather frowns and turns awkward. The announcer on the radio may speak lightly of 'scattered showers and bright periods', but this, for a crofter, may mean going over all of yesterday's work again. The drying and the 'curing' of the hay may, if the season is unsettled, be dogged by persistent showers, and the time for hay-making may drag on and on, out of all proportion to the quality and yield of the crop.

I remember one year in particular, when after a favourable spring and summer, there was promise of a good crop of grass. But disappointingly, in the hay-making season, during day after day, the weather followed the same distressing pattern. The mornings began mild, but dewy, and much too damp for the good of the lying swathes. Midday brought a fine bright sunshine, and everyone was out, visitors included, with rakes, turning, tossing and spreading the hay. Then, in the late afternoons little clouds, fluffy and innocent-looking would drift in from the Atlantic, falling as light rain. Within minutes they would have passed and be sailing over towards the mainland, with the westering sun making a series of rainbows. It was wonderful to see the clouds, showers and rainbows forming in such quick succession, the rainbows spanning the Sound like airy bridges. But to the crofter it was frustrating, standing in the lee of the lambie hoose, with the gnawing uncertainty of whether to wait until the shower was over and to try again, or whether to give it up and hope for better weather tomorrow.

Yet despite this annual struggle against rain and damp, the hay crop is usually gathered in ultimately. It is not an uncommon sight to see what looks like a cole of hay begin to move, and then to notice a pair of legs beneath it, as the crofter-wife, with her enormous load upon her back, carries it to the stackyard.

There occur, during the early weeks of autumn, phenomena called Hairst Blinks and Hairst Blash. The blinks are sudden un-expected flashes of autumn lightning, unaccompanied by storm. In themselves, these are innocuous enough, while the Hairst blash, showers of rain, short and sharp, can do great damage to standing corn and make it difficult for the reaping.

I never hear the old country dance tune 'Corn Rigs' played on the radio without picturing in my mind the little cornfields of Papa Stour. These flash upon the inward eye, Millais-like pictures of the corn, erect, gleaming and gold, or when seen from a little distance, rippling like the sea, stirred by a gentle breeze, and the silhouette of the reaper, Alex, Willie or John, dark against the pale blue of the autumn sky.

In the old days there used to be three main crops of cereals—wheat, bere, and oats—and these were ground in the small water mills, the ruins of which are still to be seen dotted about the island. It was the practice then for two or three families to share a mill.

These mills are very interesting and I always feel it is a great pity that they have been allowed to fall into ruin. Built by the men of the isle, with dry-stone walls and with turf roofs, the mills were quite small, rectangular in shape, and with a horizontally set paddle-wheel driving a vertical shaft, which in turn rotated the upper of two horizontal millstones. The power came from water diverted from the inland lochs, and when Papa Stour was more populous there were about fifteen of these mills in operation. The last one still to be used was the Muckle Mill at Da Hoops, worked by Lowery and his family as recently as in the Second World War.

Bere is still grown here on Papa Stour, by a few folk, though not in such quantities as in former times, when it seems to have been a staple. Bearded like barley, it produces a meal that is darker in colour than oatmeal and has a very distinctive flavour all of its own. There is no mistaking beremeal bannocks for ones made of oatmeal.

Just as in the voar I enjoy helping at one croft or another with the work of planting potatoes, so I get a similar pleasure in helping to gather them in at harvest time. In the spring, the feeling of newness and anticipation speeds the work along, but in the autumn there is the satisfaction of seeing the fulfilment of the season's cycle.

On an autumn day, with that special pungent tang that is all its own, it is stimulating to be out on the rig. The large baskets are already set out when I arrive, placed at regular intervals along the line of the rigs, and as the 'riping' or in-gathering begins, all the helpers work down the rows, filling the baskets. Up till quite recently the potatoes were dug out with the Shetland spade, an implement with a long wooden haft and a wooden step for the foot just above the narrow iron blade. On some of the crofts these are still used. The team work soon develops, and follows the age-old pattern, and as the work progresses the baskets fill up and are carried away.

Waiting for a new relay of empty baskets, my thoughts ran on the great dependence of the islanders upon the potato crop, and I cast my mind back to other years, when in July, in a wild spell of weather, the salt spray blown right across the island blighted and 'burned' everything in its path, including the potato haulms. Above the ground it looked as if a flamethrower had been at work. Below the ground the potato tubers were still very small, about the size of golf balls, and with the haulms gone, no further growth was possible.

This made me think of the years of desperate famine in Ireland, when the people were totally dependent upon their potato crop, and I knew now that if I was ever required to do so, I would teach that history lesson with much more conviction.

Yet in our bad year, despite the disappointment of the potato yield, we had survived, and I considered the great diversity of harvests of many lands, worked by many hands that helped to fill our larders and load our tables.

By English standards our harvest festival is always very late. Each year, I notice, it seems to take a very long time for the earth to wake from its winter sleep for any appreciable warmth to be soaked up, and the growing season is therefore late in starting. And this sets the crops a month to six weeks behind those of the south. Because of this tardiness, it has been known to hold our harvest festival services in November, and the first one in which we ever participated on Papa Stour was perhaps the most memorable.

The hay-making time that year had been dismally wet, though Jessie cheerfully assured us that next month would be better. And while the August rain soaked the rigs and ran off in muddy rivulets, there seemed to be some disparity between the prophecies of the long-range weather forecasters and what the weatherwise men on the island predicted.

September came and its equinoctial gales began early and

stretched on and on with heavy rains and a wind that battered down the standing corn. Then the islanders began talking about 'a peerie summer', a kind of Indian summer which ameliorates and temporarily holds at bay the onset of winter. We looked for it, but it never came. Instead, October, wet and cold, brought with it the rapidly shortening days. And on its last day we had our first fall of snow.

That year the Harvest Festival was on the first Sunday in November, and for the first time in our lives my husband and I, as we walked to the kirk on the previous Saturday evening, to help with the preparation and decoration, trudged through the darkness of the northern night, in deep snow.

Inside, however, the kirk was aglow. The first person to arrive had lit the two Tilley lamps and already there was a bustle of activity from the willing helpers. Peerie Mary was busy erecting sheaves of corn, twining small sprays on the rails of the pulpit and deftly placing brilliant orange marigolds among the dull gold of the bere. Lizzie, uncovering a box, disclosed varieties of godetias she had grown in a sheltered 'yaird'. And while Jessie and Helen set up turnips, cabbages and potatoes in piled up pyramids on the window-ledges, Myra arranged bread on the communion table. Mary o' Wirlie carried bright gladioli, flame, crimson and pink, which Martha had carefully tended in pots inside her porch door. Johnny had brought a lobster creel, and he, with John o' Midsetter, remembering our dependence upon the sea, as well as upon the fruits of the earth, had sent fish to represent the harvest of the sea. It is a time-honoured custom in Papa Stour to include among the harvest offerings, a glass of water and a glass of milk, both of which are basic to life and necessities, but these are usually brought in fresh on the morning of the service by Mary o' Biggins, who lives nearest to the kirk.

Before we turned down the lamps and went home, we all stood in a group at the end of the kirk and looked down the length of its aisle, and we could not but marvel at the wonder of it all. Despite the harshness of the weather, here, before our eyes, was the irrefutable proof of the ancient promise that 'while the earth remaineth seed-time and harvest shall not fail'. That year, having

72

participated in some of the work, in a small way, we felt that we could, with some justification, stand up and sing with the islanders, 'All is safely gathered in'.

But the weather in the autumn is not always rough. Calm clear days followed by sharp cold nights can be very invigorating. Sometimes on an autumn day that is bright and clear, with needle-sharp visibility, I like to watch, with a mounting sense of thrill, gannets climbing high in the pale sky, wheeling against the wind on barely moving wings, soaring in an upward vertiginous ascent, and then with swift precipitation plummeting vertically downwards, plunging into the Sound, the only sign left of their passage, a spurt of white foam.

Or early on some fine autumn morning it is pleasant to look out from one of the downstairs windows of the schoolhouse and see goldcrests perching and swinging on a thistle spike. Catching sight of my slightest movement within, or seeing my reflection on the window, they flick, startled, and fly away. They are gone, tiny flashes of green and gold, with bright orange crests.

Or walking along the side of a voe, some autumn afternoon, my footsteps, crunching on the shingle, startle a sentinel heron into flight and send it rising on broad grey wings. With slow lazy beats it goes, over the glassy waters of the voe. And so close am I that I can see its progress marked by the drops of water from its trailing legs. Or pausing on my homeward walk to look over the edge of a cliff, I can see far below me, a mother seal and her young one, the baby sleekly plump and replete, lying asleep among the boulders, while the mother swims in the shallow water close by.

Coming down Da Murrens in the gathering dusk of a late October afternoon, I see a small number of oyster-catchers, distinctively black and white, pecking among the scattered stones and broken ground with their bright orange bills. To find these birds so far away from the water's edge, comparatively speaking, is a bad sign, so folks say, presaging bad weather, gales and a stormy sea.

Quite often, in this part of the island, and at this time of the year, I catch a sound, that unmistakable cry of an otter, sharp and shrill, which is almost a whistle, but directionally as deceptive as

73

that of a ventriloquist. I know that otters do come up from the sea for fresh water to drink, and Soutra Water, a lochan nearby, and the Manse Burn which empties this into the sea at South Sands, form a convenient highway for the otters. I have seen them near the little bridge over the burn, just at the place where the stream goes under the road, and many times at dusk I have noticed their small dark shapes undulating across the open ground between Peter's gate and the burn, on their way back to the sea.

Whenever I see one of these sleek beautiful creatures my mind flies back to a fine day in spring, when Eileen, my youngest pupil, accompanied by her older brother John, arrived at the back door of the schoolhouse with a baby otter for me to see. The little creature, about the size of a small kitten, with its beautifully soft fur and appealing eyes, snuggled into Eileen's neck and obviously found great comfort in the soft wool of her Shetland cardigan. I often wonder when I see otters about Soutra Water and the burn, whether Eileen's foundling is among them.

Other lochans, like Soutra Water, which are virtually dry in the summer, fill up with the autumn rains, and these, because they are intermittent, do not always appear on maps of the island. So although humans might be misled by a blue spot on a map which cannot be correlated to the actual landscape or, conversely, by a stretch of water which cannot be located on a map, wild life is not deceived. As the hollows fill up with rain and lochans form, the creatures move in. An intermittent lochan below Da Biggins, which appears as green and lush grazing in the summer, fills up with water and provides a resting place for a family of swans and a temporary home for wild duck and geese. The same is true of Torrieshüns on the west side of the island. In the summer a green stretch of level, fine, smooth turf resembling a cricket pitch gives place, in the autumn, to a rectangular lochan where wild life abounds.

So there are many changes in the wild life as the migrants leave, and other creatures take their place, but the biggest change of all, as the year slips rapidly downhill, is the change in the length of the daylight. If the time of da hümin or twilight had to be plotted on a graph, it would in autumn most surely make a swift plunge, a sudden parabola. The way the twilight falls in the autumn, in contrast with what happens in the springtime, is best described in the old island couplet:

'In the Voar it comes creeping o'er the moss,
In the Hairst it comes galloping on a horse.'

It always seems to me that whatever the calendar tells, the last day of October marks the end of autumn and the beginning of winter. The thirty-first brings Hallowe'en and its attendant celebrations. The party for the schoolchildren follows the usual pattern, with the traditional bobbing for apples and ducking for them. Making masks beforehand is usually an easy matter and one which creates much laughter. But the manufacture of a model witch and broomstick presents problems. With no bushes or trees indigenous to the island, I have often been hard pressed to find material suitable for the broomstick. Finally I have had to resort to using thick docken stalks.

One island tradition which was practised on Hallowe'en is called Kale Throwing. It was entirely new to me, and took me completely by surprise. Long after the Hallowe'en party was over, and the children had been safely escorted home, loud bumps were heard on the back door. On investigating the mystery, my husband found a bundle of kale stalks tied to the door knob. From the darkness came sounds of subdued laughter. When this was repeated at our second back door, my husband found a few of the schoolboys, who explained that the whole trick was to tie up the kale, swing it lustily and make a resounding bang, giving the people inside the house a 'gluff' or surprise. On this, our first encounter, the whole thing had fallen rather flat, as we did not know it was expected that 'the man o' the hoose' would give chase. Having shyly explained this, they went off home. Such is their unsophisticated sense of fun.

Later that evening, however, the joke was on us. It happened that the parish minister was over for a visit and had been delayed by bad weather, and was perforce staying with us overnight. We were sitting round the fire, drinking tea, when two heavy thuds were heard, this time at the front door. We looked at each other, with Kale Throwing uppermost in our minds, and up jumped my husband saying, 'I'll catch them this time', and rushing into the hall collided with the doctor who was standing on one leg, kicking off his rubber boots—the cause of the bumps.

It transpired that he had been called to a patient here, and surmising that the lull in the weather would make a good chance for the minister to return with him, had come to the schoolhouse unannounced. Their departure was hasty because the boat was waiting. An unusual thing this—to cross the Sound at night—but the moon was full, and the sky was clear of clouds, and some little time after the two had departed, we saw the boat crossing to the mainland through the silver lane of moonlight.

8 Winter's Wark

As IN THE summer it is sometimes difficult to say just exactly when the day starts and finishes, in the winter it is just as difficult to define the beginning and ending of the night.

The square of skylight is still black, and the bedroom full of a cold uninviting air, when the alarm clock announces the start of a new day. But for its strident clangour it might be still the middle of the night. Having summoned up sufficient courage to face the cold and the darkness, I can see from the kitchen window a warm glow of light in Midsetter porch, and I know that Jessie's day has started too. Sounds in the school, subdued bumps as the desks are moved, and the rattling of the stove tell me that Mary is there making the fire, so that by the time the children arrive the school will be reasonably warm.

By this time, I am able to discern through the kitchen window, dim shapes and a few vague details, the outline of the dyke and the white glimmer of Midsetter, its chimneys and byre roofs against the paling sky.

When finally the sun makes its laggard appearance, in the south-south-east, it seems as if it is too reluctant to rise, but rather rolls along the horizon, to set in mid-afternoon in the south-south-west behind the Roond Hill, a low eminence at the southern end of the island.

In order to encourage the children to be observant of natural happenings, we go out of school, well muffled up, to see the sun, to trace its low arc in the sky and to measure our phenomenally long shadows. The school chimney, tall enough in reality, has a shadow that spreads halfway across Da Murrens. When the children are free to play I know that 'Monster shadows' is the game for the day.

Within the walls enclosing the school ground, it is almost impossible to observe the true direction of the wind, because of the aerial whirlpool the walls cause. But I watch to see which way the seagulls face when they settle on the ground. Alighting on the stretch of broken ground where last year's bonfire was, they come to rest, facing into the wind, and this tells me what I want to know. For the direction of the wind is of great importance, and determines very often what it carries with it in the matter of rain and snow, and, to a large extent, it dictates the activities of the island. Speaking very broadly the southerlies bring rain, grey veils of it trailing the showers, or heavy black nimbus clouds over-shadowing everything; whereas the northerlies may bring snow.

Born and brought up in a windy place, I thought I knew quite a good deal about the elements, but it was not until I came to live in Shetland that I realised the wind was such a powerful force and an enemy to be reckoned with. Even in a very simple thing like children's play, the wind is the deciding factor, for it precludes the use of skipping ropes and deflects the flight of balls. It makes the opening and closing of doors hazardous, and exit by the school-gate becomes a concerted effort by all concerned. It is quite a common sight to see the children holding hands as they walk home, not for any sentimental reason, but for the purely utilitarian one of not getting blown over. On many wild, windy days the parents have accompanied their children to school, in order to see them arrive in safety, and on not a few occasions my husband has escorted the bairns safely home. It is fortunate that the children themselves, while appreciating the possible danger, can see the fun of it, for, as a six-year-old wrote, 'This morning as I was coming to school I was blown off course.'

Learning to live with the wind can only be done by experience. The first essential is to have windproof clothing, for no matter how heavy or warm the garments may seem, if the texture is 'open', the wind will surely penetrate it. As well as its propensity for penetration, it has a great potential for destruction. I learnt this to my cost during a visit to Lerwick. The weather turned suddenly very rough, and being unprepared, I was obliged to buy a raincoat. No easy job this, as in shop after shop I was told that their stocks of plastic rainwear had been in great demand by visiting Russian seamen, plastics being in very short supply and much sought after in their homeland. Eventually I ran one to earth, and it lasted exactly one day. I wore it on my return journey to Papa Stour, and by the time I had called at three houses to deliver various items of shopping, my coat resembled nothing so much as a Hawaiian grass skirt. It was in shreds, not by my tearing, but by the whipping of the wind.

From the domestic angle, I soon discovered that nothing loose must be left outside or it will be blown away and come to rest up against the first fence or dyke that impedes its flight, and will remain there as long as the wind persists. I learnt that lesson the hard way, too, chasing after plastic pails.

More seriously, though, the wind can play havoc with boats. Even though they are in the noosts, the boats have to be tied down and weighted with large stones.

Early in our stay here, when we were still getting used to island living, and learning all the tricks that the weather could play, a very interesting and enlightening episode occurred.

My husband and I had noticed during that particular evening that the weather had deteriorated. At tea-time it had been just one of those grey overcast days, we thought. At supper-time a wind had sprung up, and by bedtime this had freshened considerably. My last waking thoughts that night were that the wind had become very much stronger and was rattling the slates on the roof.

Someone else on the island must have been aware of the rising wind, too—Willie o' East Toon. But unlike us, he had not remained in bed, but had done something constructive about it. In the early hours of the morning he had got up, dressed, left the house and battled his way against the wind, all the way from East Toon to South Sands, and all this in order to see if our boat was still securely tied down.

We would never have known of Willie's concern on our behalf if we had not noticed certain slight differences about the details of the knots in the ropes. When we made enquiries, it was shyly admitted by Mary, his niece, that he had been down to see if everything was all right, knowing we were newcomers and inexperienced and not yet wise to the ways of the wind.

It may sound unbelievable, but quite heavy boats have been lifted and tossed over by the wind. This happened to Peter's boat in its noost. And the wind has blown people over too. Often in the course of our travels around the island, when it has been difficult to make any headway against the wind, I have had recourse to walking immediately behind my husband, getting partial shelter. Slightly bent against the wind, we must have resembled a pantomime horse.

But the wind is not the only weather factor to be reckoned with. Awkward as the wind can be—variable, unpredictable, gusty or severe—it can also be regarded as an agent. It may, for instance, bring rain. And the two, rain and wind, working together, may bring to nought all man's schemes. An outdoor enterprise will have to be curtailed or abandoned altogether in the face of their combined onslaught. And very likely it will postpone things like visits. After a winter day of wind and rain, a crofter who has been in oilskins and rubber boots, attending to animals, will feel disinclined to stir from his own hearth in the evening.

When rain has fallen heavily for some time, filling up the hollows, the ruts made by wheels become deeper and wetter, and if cattle or ponies pass frequently over the same place, it soon becomes a sea of mud, particularly where all the paths converge at a gate. One track on the island is generally called Rotten Row, and this name is not in emulation of its London counterpart.

Struggling to the shop one winter's day, against the combined forces of wind and rain, we squelched down the sloping ground below the schoolhouse, splashed our way along the 'road' and struggled up the grassy slope called Da Scaap to Hurdiback, the shop, doing battle with two parallelogram gates on the way. We had taken our wheelbarrow, as we expected some heavy supplies. A gas cylinder was awaiting us, and when we had packed all our groceries together, there still remained the problem of a five-gallon drum of paraffin and a roll of linoleum. Outside the shop, in the growing dark, we found ourselves faced with the practical application of one of those 'what-goes-with-what' puzzles. And it finally resolved itself into the groceries being carried in a ruck-sack on my back, the paraffin and gas cylinder on the barrow, with the roll of linoleum, which seemed to be possessed of a fiendish life of its own, partially balanced, partially wedged between them.

Our journey home was a series of slithering jolts and squelchy stops when the one wheel got bogged down. The ruts and pot-holes made constant readjustments necessary to the load, but nothing seemed to stay put, being so wet and slippery with splashed mud.

It is difficult at times like this to see anything beautiful in rain. One is always inclined to take a jaundiced view of things, but there are times when, with nothing urgent in hand, a wintery shower can be a lovely thing to see: raindrops trembling on the edge of an old peat-cut, sparkling in the slanting rays of the wintery sun, flashing their prismatic colours in the pale light.

After prolonged rain, when the ground is saturated and the mossy parts like sponges, the lochans full and the burns in spate, it is possible to find in various places on the island natural pheno-mena that the islanders know as land boils. The correct geological explanation of this I do not know, but I surmise it is that the top soil is bound together by a thick matted mass of roots, and that below, is an impervious layer of rock, and between these two water collects. The effect is, when standing on it or walking across it, rather like standing on an immense rubber hot-water bottle. The size of the land boils vary very much; one near the Broch, below the Watch Hut hill, near Tiptans, covers an area about six feet in diameter, while others, like the one near Sholmach, can be anything up to fifteen feet across.

The first land boil we ever encountered caught us off guard. In the dark we purposed taking a short cut on our way home from Bragasetter, and stumbled on to it, unaware. A most disconcerting experience.

But in spite of the rain and mud, Papa Stour on the whole is naturally well drained. The burns empty away the excess water into the sea, and after perhaps two or three days, the earth begins to dry out again. And it is on days like this that I derive much pleasure in changing from the perpetual wellington boots and go out wearing leather shoes instead. There is a satisfying joy in feeling the earth firm under one's feet again, and walking becomes a pleasure once more.

A walk on a winter's afternoon can give an amazing variety of views, colours and glimpses of wild life. Even in what is often called the 'dead of winter' the island is by no means moribund.

Through the gate in the stone dyke, and on northwards, passing rocky terrain known as Greystanes, and over Birkie Shüns, an area of scattered lochans, I can look across the sea south-westwards towards the island of Foula and see it apparently floating above the surface of the water, with a line of sky seemingly visible underneath it. This optical illusion is very common in certain conditions of light and weather, and is known to the islanders as the 'yemmer'. I have seen the same illusory effect, when looking north-eastwards towards a large rocky islet called Doreholm, or seeming to cut off in a vertical way part of the northern mainland, giving it the appearance of a separate island. This faëry quality makes it like a stage setting for some phantasy.

As I walk I notice the shifting pattern of cloud that moves so fast, and changes with such an infinity of shapes, that any artist wishing to capture this on canvas would have to work swiftly indeed before the fleeting moment was, like Robbie Burns' snowflake, 'gone for ever'.

One of my favourite spots for a winter walk is Crü Barbara, with its fine beach on the west side of West Voe, and it was here that, pausing in the shelter of the ruined stone enclosure (the Crü), I watched a flock of knots, busy at the water's edge, as the tide receded. Following each little advance and retreat of the curling edge of foam, they sought for food, so many of them and so hard to distinguish in their winter plumage of two shades of grey. Further along, I could see sanderlings scurrying along the tide line, with their heads down, dabbing at small morsels left behind by the tide, their pale grey and white a very wintry colour scheme indeed.

But more wintry still, to me, was the sight of a flock of snow bunting. These had come to rest upon the broken ground to the south of Birkie Shüns, and as I approached, they rose, showing white under-plumage like a little snowstorm.

There is an old fancy that when the snow bunting comes, the snow itself is not far behind. One day we wake to find a white world. The mainland hills, Ronas Hill, and across the Sound, Sandness Hill, seem under their white covering much nearer than they really are. When the sun rises they are flushed with gold and peach, and the shadows in their corries are deeply blue. Foula, under snow, resembles an immense iced cake.

Snow lies everywhere in wind-swept curves. The harsh lines of yesterday are sculptured in smoothly rounded contours. Gateposts and fence stobs each have their own drift. Even the withered docken stalks, stubborn survivors from the summer, have a thin transparent snowy vane, filigree fine, on their lee.

In places the drifts lie thickly, and while some of the crofters clear a way from barn to byre, Muriel and her mother find that they are able to walk up their drift and over the gate. Meanwhile Alex, Jessie, Helen and Mary are busy seeking sheep buried in the snow. These have taken shelter below the very low banks near the sea. In high winds the snow is blown across in eddies, and builds up in the hollow formed by the slight overhang.

We have a similar experience to Muriel, in that we are able to walk over the school wall by means of the snow drift much more easily than digging a way through a deep drift that buried the gate. A novel way for the children to arrive at school!

Another sure place for a pile-up of snow is near the corner of the Manse Dyke. At this point, the children, after school is over, make burrows in it, like foxholes, after the manner of Desert

Rats, and the passers-by get a bombardment of snowballs in a regular enfilade.

Once, as snow lay piled up against two adjacent window-panes, a freakish wind cleared an oval shape in the centre of each pane, which looked for all the world like an enormous pair of spectacles. The same day as we noticed this, the schoolchildren discovered another comical thing in the snow. The wind had plastered snow against the corrugated iron side of the coal shed There must have been a partial thaw, followed by a very sudden freeze-up, for a curl of snow had been arrested in the act of peeling away, and stuck there, like something rolled off an enormous butter pat.

Then the children began the annual hunt for the biggest and fiercest looking icicle. They revelled in the popular game of making 'flowers' in the snow with foot patterns; standing on one leg, rotating on the heel, with the sole of the boot making the flower petal. Snowmen appeared: snowballs, each bigger and harder to roll than the last. They made snow-houses, little igloos to shelter the places where bulbs had been planted. And when all their play was over, and the sledging on the Roond Hill had finished, it was so still and calm that the sounds of Sandness came to us quite clearly on the frosty air, the noise of a car door being slammed, a dog barking in the distance, a cow lowing.

It is impossible, on a walk in December, to be unaware of the superb artistry of winter; at one moment, feeling amazed at the immensity of the scene, and at the next, marvelling at its minute perfection. Covering a huge sky canvas, winter can roll up massy clouds, piling them up like towers against the blue wash of the sky, clouds suffused with soft pink and tipped with pale gold by the weak winter sun, and all this reflecting in frozen lochans till they glow like amber.

But winter is also a master in miniatures, with countless intricate fern patterns, fine and fragile, etched in the icy surface of pools, and with a delicacy of detail feathered in the hoar frost on grass blades. The glint of the wintery sunlight reflects from a myriad tiny facets in a snowdrift, or from icicles hanging beneath a peat bank.

Perhaps the most wonderful part of winter's artistry lies in the magical way it can transform things. A weather-beaten fence post takes on a sheen of grey satin smoothness; an old stone dyke, glazed with frozen snow and polished by the wind, resembles a bank of monster sugared almonds. Dutch Loch, windswept and suddenly frozen, becomes, overnight, a mass of frosty ruffles; while Hamna Voe, in a rare frozen stillness, is transformed into a pale green mirror of the winter sky.

When we first came to live in Shetland, we received many letters expressing surprise and a certain amount of dismay, full of enquiries as to whatever we should do with our long winter evenings. The answer was simple. The winter evenings may be dark, but they are certainly not long, not long enough for all that we find to do. Never yet have we found time hang heavily upon our hands. Activities, directly or indirectly connected with my husband's work or mine, entirely fill some evenings. Then, simply because island life lacks the slick amenities of the city, the very process of living takes much time. There are no easy ready-made meals from the well-stocked supermarkets, no travelling shops at the door, no launderettes, and it goes without saying, there is no dining out. In this 'do-it-yourself' island, what has to be done has to be done by yourself. So the evenings often have a variety of chores, the overflow of the day. A surprising amount of time is taken up in correspondence of different sorts. All the business transactions, the great majority of shopping, and the paying of bills have to be done by post.

For the crofters, winter evenings are full too. When the clocks were altered for winter-time, this seemed to be the accepted signal for the womenfolk to get out their knitting needles and wool. After all the outdoor work is over for the day, the lamp is lit and the fire banked up and the women fasten on their knitting belts around their waists. These leather belts each have an oval leather pad, into which one end of the double-pointed knitting needle is placed. It supports the needle and the work is held forward instead of under the arm. In next to no time at all the fingers are flying along the 'sweerie gying' or first row. The speed of the knitting never fails to amaze me, whether it is in one of the fine patterns that Lizzie works into a lacy cardigan, or the cockle-shell pattern that Mary o' Wirlie favours for her scarves, the intricate border with which old Mrs. Robertson finishes a baby shawl, or one of the traditional designs of Jessie, Helen or Peerie Mary. The needles flash, the fingers fly and the garment grows almost perceptibly before the eyes. Working with many different colours of wool at the same time never seems to make a tangle, and what would end up as a 'cat's cradle' with an amateur, always produces under their skilful fingers beautiful symmetrical patterns.

It is a custom here, if one visits a neighbour on a winter's evening, to take one's knitting along. Anyone who did not would be thought to be 'hand idle'. So I have fallen in with island ways and take my knitting too. This is known as 'takking your sock aboot', even if the garment on the needle is not necessarily footwear. 'Sock' seems to be a general term.

One evening each week during the winter months is set aside for the Women's Guild. This is a very lively branch of the work of the Church of Scotland. I imagine that, although the aim of the Guild is the same throughout the length and breadth of Scotland, the actual meeting varies a good deal from place to place, according to local circumstance. Placed as we are, geographically remote, it is not possible to arrange for visiting speakers to lecture on different aspects of church life. Nor is it possible to have 'live' contacts with other guilds. The meeting is always opened with prayer and readings from the Bible. After this, it has become customary over the years to have a good book read aloud, in serial form, and during this part of the evening the ladies knit nonstop. Time for discussion, a break for refreshment, Guild news to be shared, and the evening closes with a benediction. These evenings with their cheerful companionship make a good chance for people in an isolated place to get together. Their daily work, by its very nature, is often a lonely business.

The menfolk here have no set organised activities in the winter evenings, yet nevertheless they do plenty of work. This is true especially before Christmas. But one winter they had a ploy of a very unusual sort. The kirk in Sandness was being wired for electricity and had gas fittings which were no longer required.

Very generously these were offered to the Papa Stour kirk to replace our Tilley lamps. Geordie (Mary o' Wirlie's father), John o' Midsetter and Johnny transported all the pipes and fittings across the Sound. There followed several nights of effort on the part of the men in a 'do-it-yourself' gas-fitting operation, fixing, screwing, testing, readjusting, until every joint and tap was tight. Then came the day when it was coupled up to the cylinder, and at last the moment of the big switch-on arrived. Every globe was lit, and where previously there had been only three lamps, each with its own pool of illumination, now there were two rows of brilliant lights. Standing looking down the aisle at them, I thought of the runway at London Airport.

Among the ageing population of the island, there are several people who are housebound. And as they cannot get to the church, the church must get to them. To this end, my husband has arranged what he calls 'Home Services', of necessity, shorter than a Sunday service in the kirk, but linking the old folk up with the wider fellowship of the church in order that they should not feel forgotten. Obviously all these services cannot be done on Sunday, and it has been arranged by mutual agreement for these home services to be conducted in the evenings during the week.

On one of these occasions we set off from home one winter's night not long ago. This particular Wednesday night was wild, stormy and cold, but a pale moon was shining wanly over the Sound. The severity of the wind made it a struggle to round the corner of the schoolhouse, gusty blows that nearly took the breath away. Outside the school walls, it was a steady hard push, until we came to the lee of the manse dyke, where we had a momentary pause for breath. Then across the open ground again, leaning on the wind, down the Barnie Houlls, the dim shape of the kirk looking solitary and deserted, with a cold spectral light upon the roof. Beyond it we could see a wraith-like spray moving over Kirk Sands. Past the Biggins dyke and up to the gate, where we struggled with the latch, against the wind, then on into the porch, using the south door on a night like that, when the wind lay in the north-west. Shedding our heavy coats and wellington boots in the porch, the door of the ben-end was opened and we had a sight that was unforgettable in its contrast with the cold world outside.

A little cameo of brightness and warmth. The room was filled with a cheerful light, the stove was glowing red; gay mats and bright cushions added more colour. Muriel, sitting near the 'bed in the wa', smiled up from her knitting; Willie with a spool of bright orange courlene at his feet was netting a lobster creel, resting this on his knee; Katie, coming forward with outstretched hand, made us welcome. And, there in the corner, sat the little old lady for whom the service was arranged, smiling and smoothing her apron in her own characteristic way. To complete the homely picture, two dogs lay asleep by the stove, and a cat upon the creepie. I reflected, for a moment, on the old lady's ninety-odd years of accumulated experience and wisdom, and the uncomfortable question rose in my mind—'Who were we, half her age, to speak with any authority?'

Some time during the evening the wind must have fallen away, because when we came out of the porch, braced to meet the blast, it was comparatively calm, and showed every sign of a coming frost. The sky had cleared and as we walked homewards, stars glinted frostily blue, red and green, and in the pools on the track we saw the reflections of Orion and his starry girdle, while behind us, in the north, flickered the first lights of the 'merry dancers'—Aurora.

9 Junketings

ALTHOUGH IN ISLAND living there is a great element of 'life is real, life is earnest', this is more than balanced by the lighter-hearted moments. In spite of the idyllic representation of Arcadia, work on the land and work on the sea, can be, and very often is, repetitive, and to some degree monotonous, and in adverse weather conditions distinctly uncomfortable. It is in the long tedious jobs that a sense of humour helps. A joke shared can make the hoeing of a long rig seem much shorter, and the remembered incident, chuckled over, will relieve the monotony of a long wearisome trudge through the rain to the pier.

We are blessed here, having a few 'wags' on the island; people who can be relied upon to give a witty reply, to crack a joke and to raise a laugh. As well as leavening the lump of heavy toil, they are valuable assets at island socials, and help to make any evening go with a swing.

A thing that struck me very forcibly when I first came to live on Papa Stour was the fact that everyone, men and women, worked so hard, and also played hard. If they were vigorous in their work, they were exuberantly energetic at a social.

As I have mentioned before, there is no public hall on the island, and any communal function has to take place in the schoolroom, whether this be a meeting of crofters, a sale of work or an address by the prospective parliamentary candidate. So it can be imagined that the schoolroom has to be prepared for a wide variety of activities.

The schoolroom is so situated and its windows so arranged that their light, either direct or reflected, can be seen from practically every house. Thus has arisen the practice that people wait in the shelter of their own houses until they see the light in the school. This is an accepted signal that things are about to happen.

In our early days here we were not aware of this, and on the occasion of the first social we were waiting in the house for someone to arrive before lighting the lamp in the school. As the time ticked away and no one came, we began to wonder if anything had gone amiss with the arrangements. In due course there came a knocking on the back door of the schoolhouse, and, upon opening it, we saw Victor standing there panting, having run all the way from the Wirlie Hoose, with a message from George, asking us to light the lamp, and adding that George would be along with his fiddle and the others would come as soon as the cow was milked.

Our source of illumination in the school in those days was a Tilley lamp, which had to be primed with methylated spirit and then pumped furiously. Once this was done, the lamp was hung on a wire suspended from the high ceiling. The signal worked. No sooner had the room its illumination than our nearest neighbours began to arrive, and others followed in rapid succession. The tiny cloakroom soon filled, with everyone removing their coats and changing their shoes. Mary o' Wirlie came in with milk for the refreshments (this time in a lemonade bottle), but still warm from the milking. George was already tuning his fiddle, the few preliminary chords, so stirring and anticipatory that I knew he had found the quickest and surest way of emptying the cloakroom. Without more ado, sets were formed for the opening dance, the eightsome reel, and this went at such a pace and with such verve that there was no doubt in anyone's mind about the success of the evening.

My memories, as I look back on that evening, are of gaily whirling figures, an ever-changing pattern of circles and lines, arches and grand chains, partners swinging round, moving on, only to meet again, the girls in colourful dresses and lacy Shetland cardigans.

As the tempo of the dancing increased and the temperature rose, I noticed the menfolk went to the cloakroom at frequent intervals to peel off a layer, first a jacket, then a pullover, until by the time the windows were a-trickle with condensation, most of them were in their shirtsleeves. As the Dashing White Sergeant's sets of six broke up and gave way to a Barn Dance, and then couples took the floor for the Gay Gordons, no one had noticed the gradual dimming of the light. The lamp, which had seen better days, had developed a leak in the pressure system and needed to be pumped up at regular intervals. One of the men left the dance, grabbed a chair, balanced precariously on it, pumped furiously at the lamp for a minute or two then, jumping down, rejoined the dance which had gone on without interruption.

It was a very refreshing thing, in these days of segregation on the basis of age, to find that people of all ages could share an evening's enjoyment. The older folk, sitting round the perimeter of the room, were finding as much pleasure in watching the young folk as the young ones were in the actual dance. The older schoolchildren joined in the easier dances, and mistakes were a source of amusement rather than of annoyance, and despite the knots in the wooden floor, sticking up like buttered brazils, they managed to dance the steps very well.

Until quite recently, the question of illumination has presented somewhat of a problem for any activity held in the school in the evening. And it has very largely precluded anything in the nature of film shows. Because of this lack of power, we have not been able to avail ourselves of the Highlands and Islands Film Guild shows. But a showing of film slides was possible, by a little ingenuity and much co-operation from John o' Midsetter and Johnny. An old twelve-volt car battery, left behind by one of our predecessors, was examined and found to be reclaimable. The big snag was to get it charged. This was where the team work came in. Johnny transported it in his trailer to the pier, and John o' Midsetter took it across the Sound and arranged for its transport to a garage in Lerwick, where it was refilled and recharged. When it was returned to Papa Stour, the show had to be held that night, as the battery, although recharged, was so old and dilapidated that it would not hold its charge for longer than twenty-four hours. So when a film slide show was in the offing, no definite date or time could be fixed. But everyone knew that when the boat brought the battery across, the show would 'go on' that night. Considering all the difficulties entailed, this worked very well, even if the last few shots did look as if they had been taken at midnight.

The same teamwork, similar to that which made these slide shows possible, was in operation on another occasion. But this involved far more people and was a masterpiece of slick timing. It happened this way. The men of the island, at another social, had volunteered to perform the historic Papa Stour sword dance. This was to be for the benefit of the 'exiles' home on holiday and for the few visitors. It was a chance remark of mine to my husband that it might be a good idea to film it. Unfortunately there was no film in his camera, and as the dance was to take place that evening, there was no hope of getting a film by post from Lerwick. So it seemed that we were stuck, until someone had a bright idea and remembered that Willie o' Bragasetter's wife, Maggie, was over in Lerwick. She was at the outpatients' department of the hospital, but would be returning to Papa Stour late that afternoon. So, after a bit of quick thinking, the upshot of it all was that we rang a friend in Lerwick, giving her the details of the film. She sent her son to the chemist's shop, purchased the film and passed it on to the town bus driver. He, in turn, handed it on to her husband who worked at the hospital. He took it to the reception clerk at the hospital and it was duly handed over to Willie's wife. She brought it back to Papa Stour in time for the photographs to be taken at the social. We had to do a deal of ringing up the next day to thank all the 'chain of agents' for their co-operation.

We were particularly keen to have a photographic record of the sword dance, as it is so rarely performed. This dance is very unusual, almost unique. Unlike the Flamborough sword dance for eight men, this is performed by only seven men. Each man represents one of the saints of Christendom: St. George of England, St. James of Spain, St. Denis of France, St. David of Wales, St. Patrick of Ireland, St. Anthony of Italy and St. Andrew of Scotland.

Led by the fiddler, they enter the room in single file. Each wears dark trousers, white shirt and a coloured sash over one shoulder, and each carries a sword. They form up in a semicircle and stand, while St. George speaks the prologue, addressing the assembled company, introducing each saint in turn and speaking of his prowess in the knightly arts. As each saint is named, he steps forward, holds up his sword and dances a few steps. After the prologue and introductions are over, the dancers form a circle and begin to weave an intricate series of patterns and movements, stepping over the swords which link them, and going under the swords held up to form arches. This lacing and interlacing culminates in a dramatic climax when the swords are formed into a seven-pointed star, held aloft by St. George. Each man reclaims his own sword, shoulders it, and St. George recites the epilogue, after which they march out in single file accompanied by the fiddler.

The Papa Stour sword dance was recorded in full detail, speeches and all, in Sir Walter Scott's novel *The Pirate*, although it is not in all editions. The origins of this most interesting dance seem to be somewhat vague. But the prologue, in its quaint wording, stirs old memories of mummers and mumming, while it is very significant that among the saints there are no Nordic ones, and those who are represented are those from countries which might well have been concerned with the Crusades. I often wonder if there is some possible connection here, as men returning from the Crusades slowly filtered back northwards. This is just my supposition, of course, and not to be taken as authentic. The origin seems to be veiled in mystery. It is very significant that there is a dance somewhat similar in its movements and pattern at Flamborough, East Yorkshire.

After this performance, and an evening of non-stop high-speed dancing, I wondered who were saints and who were martyrs!

Although many of the local traditions here have a strong Nordic flavour, they do observe one of the most famous of Scottish traditions—the celebration of Burns' Night. With some contriving and the usual good team work and co-operation, we obtained the necessary ingredients of the customary Burns' supper, the haggis. There was, of course, no difficulty about the potatoes and turnips, for they were island produce. The ladies spent a long time that day peeling them until their fingers must have felt permanently crooked. One of the major difficulties in arranging this sort of function lies in the fact that there is no water in the school, nor any cooking facilities. Therefore everything has to be prepared in the schoolhouse kitchen, which is at the other end of the building. The refreshments have to be carried through five doors and across a little yard. And it is here, crossing this open space, where the wind attacks with unexpected fury.

In the darkness and the wind, it is no uncommon thing to find food blown off the trays. At previous socials, sandwiches took flight, sugar streaked out in the wind and any liquids disappeared from jugs in a fine spray. Learning by sad experience, the ladies now covered the trays carefully and ushered each other through the windy doorways.

Although the haggis was not 'piped' in, there being no bagpipes on the island, it was 'fiddled' in, with due ceremony, George playing 'Scotland the Brave'. My husband said Burns' own grace, and the supper followed in traditional manner, with the toasting of the Immortal Memory.

I suppose all Burns suppers, by their very nature, will have to follow a somewhat similar pattern, but from the small handful of people living here it was amazing to find the wide variety of ways in which to commemorate Rabbie . . . a short biography from George, duets from Mary o' Biggins and Lizzie; 'Ca' the Yowes', that was Alice's delightful solo, while the older folk entertained everybody by reciting many of the longer poems, like 'Tam o' Shanter', by heart.

Sitting chatting to them afterwards, while the dancing was

in progress, I was impressed by their understanding and real appreciation of Burns, and I realised more fully that, in many respects, the lives of some of the menfolk were not dissimilar to his. They lived close to the land, they were familiar with nature; they knew the unceasing battle against wind and weather; they regulated their work by the changing cycle of the seasons, and knew the rhythms of ploughing and harvest.

Taking pride in their island heritage and keen to preserve their own traditions and their history, the Papa Stour folk hold Shetland evenings from time to time. These, in a way, follow a similar pattern to a Burns Supper, but the food eaten is of old island dishes, reastit mutton (salted, dried mutton) and clapshot (a mixture of mashed potatoes and mashed turnip), bere meal bannocks and clootie puddings (a kind of dumpling containing raisins and currants, all cooked in a cloth), being the most popular. These foods were eaten regularly in the old days, before the introduction of cans, packets and 'instants', and very solid and nourishing they are. After a meal of this sort there is a marked disinclination to rise, or to participate in any violent physical activity. All one wishes to do is to sit back and watch a humorous Shetland sketch, or listen to a Shetland reading or poem.

But no one will be allowed to feel soporific for long. A fiddle will be produced and tuned up, and feet will start tapping. And as the ladies clear up the dishes in the schoolhouse kitchen and tackle a mountainous washing-up, someone will put his head round the door to say, 'Come on, the dancing has started' followed by a chorused reply, 'Yes we know—we felt it', the vibrations travelling along the joists and floorboards as the familiar rhythms are literally stamped out. Hurrying through the chores, back across the windy yard, and into the schoolroom again, the ladies are drawn into the circle of swirling figures.

Of course the activities in the schoolroom are not always so vigorous, nor so hard on the foundations. We also use the same room for more sedate functions. One event of this nature that is always welcome after the long and very dark winter is the Bulb Show. This was an inspiration on George's part, and generous too, for it is he who each year provides the bulbs, and the prizes to be won. In October each lady on the island receives a small exciting parcel containing the bulbs, and after that it is up to her to set them in as attractive a way as she can. Then follows the anticipation and the comparing of notes during the winter months. And when the day of the show has been fixed, the real anxiety starts. Someone's bulbs kept in an over-warm room are almost ready to bloom, while those of another competitor, retarded by being kept in a colder 'ben-end' of the house, have to be forced on, set in a sunny window, while another of the ladies may be convinced she will have to sit up at night to bring hers on.

On the day of the show it is interesting to observe the way the ladies get their bowls of bulbs to the school safely. To protect the flowers from the rough buffeting from the wind, many of the ladies carry their precious burdens in cardboard boxes or huge cartons obtained from the shop. The bulbs are set out, on display, with last minute titivating, and then the judging begins. The colour and beauty of the massed flowers are things to uplift the heart, and the fragrance of the hyacinths lingers long after the evening is over.

But socials, like all good things, must come to an end; and when the votes of thanks are over and the clapping is finished, it might be expected that 'Auld Lang Syne' would be sung. And indeed it is sometimes, particularly if 'exiles' are about to depart. But to my mind, the best way of all to close a social evening is to sing Papa Stour's own island song, 'Da Sang o' da Papa Men'.

DA SANG O' DA PAPA MEN

Chorus

Oot bewast da Horn o Papa,
Rowin Foula doon!
Ower a hidden piece o water,
Rowin Foula doon!
Roond da boat da tide-lumps makkin
Sunlicht trowe da cloods is brakkin;
We maan geng whaar fish is takkin,
Rowin Foula doon!

Verses

Fishy-knots wir boat haes, truly
Nae misforen knot.
We hae towes an bowes an cappies,
Ballast ida shott,
Paets, fir fire ita da kyettle,
Taaties fir da pot.

(Chorus)

Laek a lass at's hoidin, laachin,
Coortit be her vooers,
Papa sometimes lies in Simmer
Veiled wi ask an shooers;
Dan apo da wilsom water
Comes da scent o flooers.

(Chorus)

We can bide ashore nae langer—
We maan geng an try.
We'll win back, boys, if we soodna
Scrime da moder-dy,
Fir da scent o flooers in Papa
Leds wis aa da wye.

(Chorus)

In the days of the old sixaerin fishing (a six-oared boat) it was the custom to row westwards from Papa Stour until the 1300-foot cliffs of Foula were down on the horizon, this was known as 'rowin' Foula doon'.

I never hear the song sung without remembering Lowery's words to us the very day we arrived, when he told us of the scent of the Papa flowers; and each summer when I smell the air, heavy with the breath of clover, I recall that it was the self-same scent which guided home those Papa men of long ago.

10 Yule

FOR MANY CITY FOLK, the words 'Christmas Shopping' must conjure up pictures of bright lights, decorated shops, gay displays and immense quantities of goods; toys and gifts of infinite variety. But I imagine, too, these words evoke memories of crowds, bustle, slushy pavements, large stores, packed lifts and escalators, lost children and all rounded off with an uncomfortable ride home in a full bus.

But Christmas shopping is not like that for us. Nothing could be more different. Here, on Papa Stour, we have none of those things. Instead, we have the one shop which supplies everything, and the thirty folk or so who make up the entire population could never be called a crowd.

Yet for all its smallness and its lack of city glamour, Christmas shopping is fun. I often recapture some of that fun by recalling what took place the first year we were here.

Early in November we heard of things mysteriously called 'The Draperies'; a word here, a suggestion there, just enough to excite the curiosity, to titillate the imagination. This was advance publicity, island style.

In the schoolhouse, after school was over, I began to deal with the paraffin lamp; and my husband coming through from the front room announced brightly, 'I have just seen the boat coming.' We both went to the window. The island boat, only just visible in the mist and gathering darkness, was making its way across the Sound, and heading in the general direction of Housa Voe. It was heavily laden and low in the water. Thinking of the cargo it carried, we said simultaneously, 'The draperies!'

Without further ado we donned rubber boots and raincoats and set off with rucksack and wheelbarrow.

We saw only one person on our journey to the shop, a shadow darker than the surrounding shadows, whose progress was marked by the occasional flicker of a torch.

Leaving the road we took the short cut across the knowe to the store. That short cut was disastrous. I tore my plastic mac on the stile and flapped into the shop doorway like the loser in a dipping-lug race. We parked the wheelbarrow and opened the shop door.

Going into that shop worked a complete transformation on us both. The slight mishaps of the way were forgotten in the scene that was before us. For my part I felt as if I had been pitchforked into a theatrical set of a village comedy, and suddenly I was not a spectator but a participant in its light-hearted fun.

To say the shop was full was a real understatement. There were bodies and goods everywhere. In addition to the normally well-stocked shelves, there stood a large number of containers, like suitcases without handles; these, then, were 'The Draperies'.

What magical ideas I could conjure up in those two words— The Draperies! Words subtle and evocative, they had finally materialised and become substance. All the mystery of the East lay in those handle-less suitcases, the very stuff of the Orient, and seven-veiled dancers.

Alex, the shopkeeper, decided that it was dark enough to merit the lamp being lit, but what with the gusty draughts whenever the door opened, the swinging of the suspended lamp and waiting for the burner to heat up, the process of illumination was somewhat lengthy.

I was wondering somewhat anxiously where the fabulous draperies would be displayed. There was simply not an inch of room on the counter. Several piles of groceries, two shopping bags, newspapers and periodicals, brass weights and paper bags filled the entire space. Floor space was just as limited, there were nine persons altogether, one cat and one dog. 'The draperies, oh! the draperies,' I was thinking, longing to see these exotic goods. Someone else must have been thinking along the same lines, for I heard a voice say, 'Now about the draperies. Might I be looking at a few while you are reckoning up my bill?' Alex agreed. This idea of selling two lots of goods at the same time could be called high-pressure salesmanship, island style.

Forthwith, the uppermost of the handle-less suitcases was lifted over the heads of the customers, and after a concerted raising of arms and a perceptible ducking of heads, everyone craned forward to see the locks released and the draperies revealed.

A mass of custard-pink stays, with cruel-looking laces, lay in their brazen nakedness without any scrap of cellophane to shroud them. Someone cleared his throat and there was a world of meaning in the sound.

Without comment Alex plunged his hand deeply in the case and hauled up a quantity of headscarves. They were of garish colours, with flowers so large as might only be seen in Kew or Chelsea. The customer seemed interested, so they were pushed further over the suitcase for closer inspection. One was opened completely, then bunched up in a loose knot to give it a realistic appearance. While the customer was making up her mind, Alex had other things to do. He moved off to the bread boxes and began ripping off the covers. Having selected two brown loaves, he wrapped them and handed them over my head to the youth behind me. He departed, and his exit was marked by a violent gust from the door. The lamp flickered, and while someone reached to pump it up, the miniature mannequin parade of head-scarves was still going on. A second case was lifted over our heads and put on top of the first. More draperies.

This time, a quantity of boys' and youths' shirts were displayed. These were of the cowboy type—checks, fringe and all. And their eruption from the box was followed by 'oohs' and 'ahs' all round. Several shirts were tried up against the outstretched arms of a little duffle-coated lad, and he stood there, somewhat self-consciously, while comments were made on the size, quality and colour.

Another box of draperies was passed overhead, and still another. And one customer, with a great quantity of garments over her left arm, was reaching up again and again to the uppermost case, well above her eye-level, for more. But this must have been somewhat in the nature of a lucky dip, pulling first a strap here, a tape there or a lace edge, till finally the whole garment would slither down and come to rest, a shapeless pile of artificial silk, on top of her other purchases. Then the garment would be shaken out and held up as she stood screwing up one eye as if picturing some human form inside it, measuring, sizing and estimating. Another customer was looking at aprons, another riffling through pairs of socks, while men's ties were being looped round various fingers. In the angle of the counter someone was vainly struggling with an enormous bath towel, trying to persuade it into its original folds.

Within the small compass of the shop there was movement and colour, a tangle of stretching, lifting and measuring, a blaze of gay stripes, bright 'florals' and splashes of reds, blues and greens to dazzle the eyes. And laughter—it was abounding, as garments, comical, ultra-modern or quaint were offered for sale to unlikely customers. From 'The Draperies' which had, in my fancy, sounded sublime, we had descended to the ridiculous.

Finally we were served. Our rucksack was filled, as was the barrow. And as we trundled it home in the windy dark, we envied the city folk nothing of the bright lights and glamour. We had had our own brand of enjoyment.

In this world of change, where nothing stays the same for very long, even Papa Stour in its remoteness is not entirely unaffected. Due to internal changes, the method of Christmas shopping in subsequent years was completely altered. When the shop changed hands and moved its premises, a new style of Christmas shopping was introduced. Myra, who took over the shop, ordered goods from Lerwick tradesmen, as Alex had done, but she found her premises were not big enough to set out the goods for all to see. So, after consultation, the schoolroom was pressed into use in yet another capacity, that of a shop.

As with all functions in the school, the lighting of the lamp was the signal that the shop was open, and within a few minutes the first customers arrived. This shop was not just a 'one-night stand', but remained open for a week, during the evenings only, all the goods being repacked and the tables cleared in preparation for the next day's school.

To children who could count their visits to the town on the fingers of one hand, and who had never seen a large city store decorated for Christmas, this festive display was a revelation. Watching the children's enjoyment was more of a pleasure to me than the actual shopping. To see them walking round the tables, looking at everything with incredulity and wonderment would have opened the eyes of many a blasé city dweller. Round and round the displays the children went, and when, at last, they were bedazzled with so much variety, colour and brightness, they sat down on a form and enjoyed a harmless little joke. They each found a large brown paper bag and extinguished themselves.

An alternative method of Christmas shopping, which however has drawbacks, is to go personally into Lerwick. This necessitates a journey by boat, and an even longer journey by hired car, and because of the short daylight hours it almost always means staying overnight. There can be further complications when having done the intended Christmas shopping, the weather turns awkward and renders the journey back across the Sound impossible. This sort of thing is by no means uncommon—to be 'storm-stayed' on the mainland. It seems that Lizzie holds the record for this, being stranded in Sandness for ten days.

The remaining alternative is Christmas shopping by mail order catalogue. And this seems to be the method most used nowadays. Flicking over the glossy and seductive pages of the catalogues— armchair shopping—is very easy for the customer, but in reality, whether the goods come from a mail order stores catalogue or by post from the shops in Lerwick, it all falls on the willing shoulders of John o' Midsetter. In good weather it is very cheering to see the little boat coming across the Sound, heavily laden, and the pleasant anticipation of receiving the goods one has ordered by post fills one with pleasure.

But what goes on between the time when I first sight the boat and the time when I receive my quota of mail is interesting. The boat goes to the pier, or if the weather is inclement, to Cullivoe, where the anchorage is safer. John unloads all the bags, and shoulders them to the post-office, a back-breaking job. In bad weather, in the winter, in storms or doubtful spells of weather, when the radio forecast predicts squalls or changeable winds, John has a stretch of rough country to negotiate. In the weeks preceding Christmas, John's work is particularly hard. Rough weather and high winds make it difficult enough, but late morning light and early evening dark shorten the day when a crossing of the Sound can be effected. And it is at this time that the mails are the heaviest. Goods ordered by post, bulky objects bought from mail order catalogues, all have to be carried on John's shoulders. And, often, from my kitchen window, I watch a figure coming over the sky-line, heavily laden with what is virtually other people's shopping.

It is not a very far cry from Christmas shopping to Christmas itself, and once people begin to talk about Yule (as Christmas is known here), there is a perceptible quickening of the tempo of living. The intervening weeks seem to pass very quickly. One thing which occupies a great deal of time is preparing for the annual concert. This is a time-honoured institution, and, as in many other things, it is a 'do-it-yourself' effort. And that goes for everything: the stage, the décor, the acts, the music and the 'props'.

Like all social functions, the concert has to take place in the school, and in order that the performers should be seen to better advantage, Johnny had a bright idea of making a stage out of salvaged fish-boxes. Scrubbed, cleaned and inverted, they were set together for our first concert and everyone seemed to think that this innovation was a good one. They were just the right height for the audience; there was no craning of necks, and they were not too high to climb upon. They were fine—until, during a solo item, the young lady performing, putting her all into a heart-rending song, stepped back rather dramatically and spoilt the whole effect when her stiletto heel stuck into a knot-hole.

From then, each year, there have been developments in stage craft. Johnny produced a roll of linoleum to cover the boxes, obviating any further let-downs. One year a proscenium arch and front was constructed from hardboard. Another year, curtains were made, and pulleys, brackets and all were of home manufacture. The lighting presented a difficulty, and because of the awkwardness of the Tilley lamp, there could be no professional dimming or special lighting effects. Yet, with ingenuity and some contriving, shadow-shows were put on as part of the entertainment, especially for the children's benefit. They certainly succeeded, if success can be judged by the fact that one little boy in the audience fell off his seat laughing.

Humour is a great ingredient of the concert, but local lore, old island tales and sketches all have their place. And the Shetland readings and dialect verse never fail to entertain. In such a small community, we are very fortunate to have people amongst us who are of a resourceful turn of mind. Johnny, with his guitar, can improvise an accompaniment at very short notice; Jessie, Helen and Katie can be relied upon to cast about for interesting and amusing dialect items, while John o' Midsetter is a master at the art of producing stage furniture. I bring to mind a particularly realistic Rayburn stove which might well have fooled an expert. George, with much serious poetry to his credit, can create items that range from local legends dramatised into sketches, to humorous songs which he performs himself, poems for his sister, Mary, to recite, and lovely prose pieces that are both reflective and evocative.

Sometimes when I have a turn-out at school, many nostalgic memories are stirred by the sight of some of the old 'props' stacked behind a bookcase, forgotten; a section of a castle wall painted on lino, a Gothic window manufactured from a large cardboard carton, two plywood swords, a cocked hat, masks, a monstrous dungeon door key cut out of hardboard, and other bric-à-brac: the shades of plays and players lingering on the stage of memory.

The real start of the Yule festivities is the carol singing on Christmas Eve. The younger folk form a party, mustering about a dozen, and, equipped with carol sheets and torches, they set off from their assembly point at the schoolhouse and make their way to the Wirlie Hoose. There, the numbers grow, when George and Mary join the party, George with a storm lantern. With the addition of another strong male voice, not only is the volume of singing increased, but the morale of the little company gets a boost. In this 'Round the Island' carol singing, every house is visited, and the usual route goes from the Wirlie Hoose at the south end via the Post Office, Midsetter and Peter's house, and thence to the cluster of houses by the kirk, all known as the Biggins. Up till then, the going is not usually too difficult. Most of the way is by the track or well-known paths and with fairly easy gates to negotiate. Then the torches and storm lantern come into their own, as the group makes its way to Hurdiback, up the grassy slope and over the wire fences. But this is just the beginning of what can be described as an 'adventure playground'—skirting Housa Voe, passing the lochan, up the sharp incline to East Toon and down again, over the broken ground below the kirk, there to regain the track.

Looking back over the Christmas Eves we have spent here, the one word that looms large is weather. We have had Christmas Eves of light drizzle, when woollen scarves and fur gloves have been damply unpleasant to the touch; wet ones, when our hymn sheets have ended up a soggy handful, not far removed from papier-mâché, and we, in glistening oilskins, were told we looked more like pot-holers than carol-singers; Christmas Eves when the dark sky was sprinkled with glittering stars and the breath hung crisping on the frosty air; a Christmas Eve when, defying the wind, we faced the driving snow and stinging hail and learnt the Shetland word for it, 'sweeing'; an unforgettable Christmas Eve of calm moonlit beauty, when roofs, lochans and voes were bathed in silver, a silver that was splintered into a thousand fragments on the surf of Kirk Sands.

But, whatever the weather chances to bring, rain, blow, murk or moonlight, there is one constant factor: the Papa Stour hospitality which remains the same, genuine, openhanded and warm.

Christmas morning brings its special church service, and walking to the kirk often seems like stepping into a Christmas card. A white world, with each gate-post and fence-stob capped with its own white cushion, and the kirk itself under a white blanket. The decoration of the kirk for Christmas could present some difficulty, as there is no holly or evergreen indigenous to the island, but well wishers in the south usually send a box of greenery and the little kirk takes on a festal appearance.

As the old year ticks itself away, there is still plenty of activity. The children prepare to go guising on Old Year's Eve. Dressed in weird costumes, and masked, they visit every house, and present themselves for everyone's inspection and amusement, maintaining an absolutely strict silence. Their complete disguise and perfect masking leave only their eyes as a means of identifying them, but the youngsters know this, and when any grown-up approaches them, they shut their eyes to preclude recognition; then they leave, usually well rewarded for their silent mumming show.

The grown-ups are busy too, in a variety of ways. On the last night of the year, some go to the Watchnight Service, and afterwards, with much handshaking and well-wishing, the New Year is rung in on the kirk bell. Others may be preparing for the arrival of the first-footers, stirring up the fire and setting out the refreshments. And while some of the younger men exuberantly discharge a few shots into the air, one man (Geordie) will be busy signalling, in Morse, with a flash-lamp to his relatives across the Sound, his message—'A Happy New Year'.

11 Legends, Lore and History

I HAVE OFTEN heard it said that the history of a village is written in its church, and that upon its churchyard stones the long chronicle of life is recorded in the names to be found there. With Papa Stour, much of its history can be traced through the fascinating place-names on its map.

In what dim age, I often wonder, did people first dwell here? There are more than a few traces of ancient habitations, and my mind flies backwards over the centuries as I lean a hand on an ancient stone, and I wonder whose hand first wrested it from the earth and placed it in position to make the foundation for a dwelling. But this is not wholly my fancy; there is visible proof that Stone Age peoples lived here and built their wheelhouses. Near Cullivoe, where we held our John's mass banket, these early peoples lived, and perhaps it was a deeper sense, other than those of mere sight and hearing, that made me aware of the 'dawn of time' that June daybreak. And as my thoughts ran on, I wondered what feet, other than ours, had climbed that headland; what eyes had scanned the same seas; what figures, bent almost double under their heavy loads of stone, had toiled where we played;

what silent watcher by the shore had stood with fish-spear poised, motionless; what patient worker chipping stone on stone had fashioned his tools, not half a spear's cast from where we sat.

And the Broch? That strange enigma. A name on a map, and a name frequently on people's lips, yet no trace of a building survives, save for an arc of stones revealed at low tide. This is a mystery I often ponder on, imagining a broch standing, sheltered from the wind by the hill behind it, and impregnable, with the sea on its other three sides. Yet it vanished, and only the name remains.

It is easy to understand how some of the place-names came about; for example, South Sands, North Banks, Round Hill, East Toon, a toon being a settlement or group of houses, but did Queediness appear as a white headland? However, some of the names are not so obvious in their derivation. Verdifield has really nothing to do with verdure or greenness, but is a corruption of Ward or Watch, and, being the highest hill on the island, would be the obvious place for a look-out post. I have heard it explained that Girsindie Geo meant girse (or grass) in the geo. But, after consulting higher authority, I learn that a Gor was a dyke, and that this particular dyke ended at the geo. It was literally the Gor's end; but through corruption or careless speech became Girsindie Geo. And if klunger means a briar rose, were there ever briar roses in Klingri Geo?

We often get enquiries about the name of the island itself, how it should be pronounced, and what it means. Some visitors give it the slightly Victorian flavour of Papá, with the accent on the second syllable, whereas it should be on the first, and so pronounced Paa-pa Stoor. (This is the nearest I can give it in writing.) Its meaning, the large Priest Island, would suggest that there had been a religious foundation of some sort when the Norsemen came. Most of the island's place-names are of Norse origin, and this seems to suggest that, not only were they the dominant people, more in number and bigger in physique and more highly developed, but that they ousted any previous names, and named the island of their choice with their own Norse words. And it is those names which have survived.

Names which always sound very Norse to me are Hamna Voe, Olie's Voe, (the old name for West Voe), Oligarth, no doubt, Olaf's garth; the well that has the reputation of never running dry is Klinkhamar; Swarter Skerry, the black skerry at the mouth of Hamna Voe, Skarvitaing and Fiskitaing, a taing being a point of land, Snuyens and Valsness on the eastern side of Papa Stour—all these have a very strong Norse ring about them.

One mystery is of the name of Galtigeo, reputed to mean the geo of the pig, yet pigs are known here as grise.

The hill at the south end of the island, behind the Wirlie Hoose, is known as Hilla-fielly, and it seems to be commonly held that this name means Holy Field. The word very often used for Sunday is the Helly. But other people have expressed another theory, that the word Helly is used in the same sense as it appears in Up-Helly-Aa, the Norse festival of light, and in the German 'hell' light or bright. I am inclined to think that there may be something in this idea. I have never found anything that I would consider particularly holy on the hill, no remains of ecclesiastical settlements, no hermit's cell; indeed no such remains have been found on the island, but this hill is used as a gauge for the sun, in its seasonal movements. In the winter, the sun never rises above it, but as the year progresses the sun works round the hill and rises above it in an ever-increasing arc. There is another theory that a small religious settlement may have been there, which was used subsequently by the lepers.

Some of the house names and croft names are equally interesting. Quite a few of these bear the suffix 'setter', a word of Norse origin, implying a small settlement of two or three houses. So, there is Bragasetter, Midsetter, and West Midsetter. Hillydales, which on first hearing sounds a contradiction in terms, may possibly be a corruption of Hellydale, and certainly it is in a light and bright position. But a far more likely explanation is that it is derived from, and is a corruption of, the Norse, meaning Flat Rocks and Rigs. The names of Da Scaap and Hurdiback remain somewhat enigmatic, though it may be that Da Scaap meant a place of shallow soil, another derivation from the Norse. The three remaining houses, of a collection near the kirk, known as Da

Biggins, seem to have derived their names from the verb 'to big' or 'to build'. Very little seems to be known about a remnant of a building there, still called Da Sweerie Haa (or the First Hall), but who built it and who dwelt there and how it came to be in ruins, no one knows.

All of these houses and crofts lie on the fertile area east of Scattald Dyke. There are, however, the remains of two houses west of this dyke. One which was inhabited within living memory is the croft of Hamna Voe, and I often picture the scene as it would be, about eighty years ago, as the family of children were rowed across the voe to shorten their journey to school. The only other dwelling, also ruined, west of Scattald Dyke, stands on the west shore of Cullivoe, and about it there is an air of mystery, Tulloch's büde (or booth), but who Tulloch was and what happened to him and his, not even the old folk remember. Now, in its silence, the rabbits and the wrens are its only inhabitants; the nettles and the thistles grow waist-high in the broken doorway, and moss creeps over the sill.

But probably the most interesting dwelling from a historic point of view is Tirval's Skord, though only the site of the house remains. This was the home of Lord Thorwald Thoresson, who was an agent of the then Norwegian royal family, and was a collector of taxes for them. Incidentally it is through him that the history of Papa Stour was first documented, for in 1299 there was an enquiry held, which subsequently cleared him of all suspicion of malpractices and fraud. But his name lingers on here in quite another connection. There is a high stack, near the 'Pass' at the entrance to Housa Voe, which bears the name of Maiden Stack, or Frau Stack. Folklore has it that Lord Thorwald had his daughter immured upon it to keep her safe from the unwelcome attentions of possible suitors. Legend also has it that the stack was climbed and the lady rescued by some enterprising young man. Whatever the truth of it is, there is visible today evidences of a small stone cell.

Two other stone curiosities which always intrigue visitors to the isle are the Giant's Stone, a large boulder at the North end, and the Giant's Grave, on the top of the Roond Hill. I suppose many rural places boast of their past giants and big men, and legends of their feats of strength abound. One such giant, in Papa Stour, is reputed to have thrown two stones into the sea. Both stones lodged fast and became Forwick Holm and Melby Holm, little islets in Papa Sound. This is obviously pure legend, but it is interesting to link these with the knowledge that the incoming Norsemen of superior physique would appear to be giants to the stocky little Picts. Lore suggests that as the Norsemen settled and claimed the isle and all that was in it, the Picts were reduced to living on the western side, in and around the caves, and existed by making nocturnal raids on the homesteads or setters of the Norse invaders, retrieving what they considered to be their own and thereby giving rise to the stories of the Trows (like the Norwegian Trolls).

A series of little water mills, all now in ruins, bear the name of Trowie Mills. These actually were operated by water from the Loch of Selligeo. But legend has it that the Trows still use these mills, but only at night, very carefully reducing them to ruins again, each day, before dawn.

To the south of these mills there is a wild and rather barren stretch of country which is criss-crossed by the remains of a number of most ancient stone dykes. The origin of them has been lost in the mists of antiquity. The mysterious thing about them is that they seem to mark no obvious boundary, but sprawl haphazardly all over the area. What their original purpose was is extremely difficult to say.

To those who are sensitive to atmosphere and who are receptive of things other than those perceived by eye and ear, there is one particular place on the island which has a mysterious magnetism. This is Miley Punds, designated on the map as a 'deserted village'. In actuality, it consists of a few lichened grey stone enclosures, in a small green saucer of land. Though ruined, it is not melancholy; though deserted, it is not forlorn. As the sun slides behind the encircling hillocks and the blue shadows fall athwart the clearing, one becomes vaguely aware of 'presence', and there is a sensation of rubbing shoulders with history.

There must have been some noteworthy personalities in the

past, people who, for one reason or another, left their mark in place-names in various parts of the island. I think of Wilma Skerry, Crü Barbara and Kirstane's Hole, but who these three ladies were no one has any idea, nor why their memory should have been perpetuated. One of the big sea caves is called Francis Hole, while a headland in the north bears the interesting name of Jerome Coutt's Head. There is Willie's Taing, and a particular piece, a part of West Voe, is Robbie's Noost, but their identity is lost too, as also are the reasons for associating their names with those special spots of ground. One of the quaintest place-names is Nanny Cheyne's Ship; this is a rock near Skibbie Geo which forms a convenient platform from which to fish. But who Nanny was and whether she actually fished there is not known. A relatively small sea cave at the south-west corner of Papa Stour has the delightful name of Johnny Weary's Hole, and not so far away is Muckle Karl's Geo, while beyond Kirstane's Hole is Benny Geo; but, again, there are no written records and no oral legends of the three men, Johnny, Benny and Karl. Just the names, no more. Local tradition has it that anything washed up in Benny Geo is the rightful property of the minister or missionary, but even the origin of this is not known.

However, the origin of the name of Dutch Loch is known. It seems to be a generally held idea, that in the days when the Dutch operated a large fishing fleet in Shetland waters, some of these vessels came into Hamna Voe for shelter, and the crews replenished their fresh-water stocks from the loch; they are also reputed to have washed their linen there. It is to be hoped that the laundry work went on below the point where they filled their water casks. I wondered, as I found the remnants of a wooden clog, on the shore, just how old it was, and who had worn it. This set me wondering about other things: what had the loch been called before the Dutch came? and why had this nickname ousted some former name, possibly a Norse one, when this does not seem to have happened anywhere else on the island?

A little while ago I had cause to look through some old school records, and among these, a register. My eye fell on an address, 'The Station'. This seemed so out of place, as the word is always associated in my mind with railway stations, and, of course, there are no railways in Shetland. Then I remembered the rusting remains of a pier and a few bases of buildings on the shore of West Voe; the deserted remnants of a fishing station.

In the days of the big fishing fleets of small boats, Papa Stour must have been a flourishing place. A hundred years ago the population was three hundred and fifty one. There must have been scenes of great activity as the boats, laden with their catches of herrings, came into the fishing stations at West Voe, Hamna Voe and Cullivoe. There would be work for all: the girls and women gutting, and the boys laying the fish out upon the shingle beach to dry and warding off any marauding seagulls. This period of prosperity lasted until just past the turn of the century, when the fishing fell off and the population began to decline. I like to hear the old folk of the isle talk about those days, the hey-day of Papa Stour; for these old folk of today were the self-same fisher-lassies. Although in those days they did not know of the existence of such things as vitamins, they knew all there was to know about the virtue of fish oil as an important nutritional factor in a diet which was otherwise rather low in vitamin content. As well as telling me about their fish recipes and how to make 'stap' and 'crappen'—one, a fish recipe using the head and liver of the fish, and the other fish liver mixed with oatmeal and seasoning—they also remember how they prepared the fish oil for their little colley lamps.

I can picture them in my mind, after the return of the herring boats with a good catch. There would follow a hard day's work, a long trudge home and an evening meal of tatties and herring and bere-meal bannocks. Then the lamp would be lit, the peat fire made up, and the lassies would arrive for the 'cairding'.

It was a tradition here that the younger women would go to each other's homes, by some prearranged plan, to work together, carding the wool prior to spinning. Each would arrive with her own bundle of wool from the last rooing, and her cairds. These are wooden tools about the size of a table tennis bat, but rectangular in shape, faced on one side with stiff, short bristles, to comb out the fibres of the wool until all lie in one direction. This work, which might have been tedious if done alone, went on more easily to the accompaniment of laughter and talk. When the work was done, someone would suggest a dance to round off the evening. A fiddle would be brought out and tuned up, and the feet that had stood by a gutting bench throughout the long hours of a working day, began to tread out a Shetland reel.

In the other houses, where older folk were probably looking after young children, the evenings were very different, and much quieter. The glow from the fire and the dim light from the lamp made it necessary for those who were knitting to sit in a rather tight circle round the sources of illumination, while the children sat in an outer ring, and so became known as 'peerie oot-by tings' (little outside things). Although they were sitting there, they were not excluded entirely from the company, and listening, could catch on to the wisdom of their elders. In those days when life was less sophisticated the entertainment was simple in the extreme. The older folk set the children riddles, known as guddocks, and the children had to solve them. Many of these guddocks still remain; some are quite long; many of them are rhyming, and all of them are concerned with the homely familiar things of daily living that children would appreciate—the broom, the kettle, the fire, the candle, the Kirk bell.

> Roond like a millstane,
> Lugget like a cat,
> Guess a' day
> But ye'll no guess that.
> (The iron cooking pot)

And while the mother reached for her needle and thread, she would set them another puzzle.

> Peerier or a mouse, bigger or a louse,
> Mair doors and windows, or all the King's house.
> (Thimble)—

with the answer before their very eyes. Or as someone replenishes the fire,

> Lang legs, nae knees
> Roond feet like bawbees.
>   (Firetongs)

> A marble wall as white as milk,
> All lined with skin,
> And smooth as silk;
> Neither doors nor windows
> That man can behold,
> Yet the thieves break through
> And steal the gold.
>   (Egg)

And when all the guddocks concerning homely objects have been posed and guessed, thoughts would be turned to outdoor things which everyone would have seen upon the croft.

> Lang man, legless,
> Gaed to the door staffless;
> Says, 'Good wife put up your ducks and hens,
> For dogs and cats I care not.'
>   (The worm).

> Stands on one leg,
> With its heart in its head.
>   (The cabbage)

Or sometimes, striking a more serious note, one of the older folk would ask,

> The beginning of Eternity,
> The end of time and space,
> The beginning of every end,
> And the end of every race.
>   (The letter 'E')

These and many, many other guddocks are still remembered, and I think perhaps Helen and Peter could rightly claim to be experts on this subject. Occasionally at school, while we drink milk at the mid-morning break, the children ask each other a few.

Another entertaining way of spending an evening in the gloaming was to repeat the family trees. In a small closely-knit community, this was not only interesting but very necessary, as even from early childhood they would know their own family history, back for many generations, and also close and distant relationships. Whenever I hear older folk speaking of all the ramifications of their family trees, it puts me in mind of Matthew, Chapter One.

Towards the end of the nineteenth century, life here must have been very hard, but simple and uncomplicated. There was very little contact with the outside world, and I am told that the mail delivery consisted of three or four letters and one newspaper—this for the schoolmaster, who having read it, passed it on to those who wanted it. Comings and goings were very infrequent, as those of the Papa Stour men who were deep-sea sailors would be away months, possibly years, at a time. An island lad intending to go to sea took his sea-chest and was rowed across the Sound to Sandness. There he shouldered his box and walked the twenty-odd miles to Lerwick. A Papa Stour wife who had knitted steadily all the winter, would, one day, pack up all her 'hosiery' in a bag and set off, very much the same as her husband or her son had done. The women made up a party, and walked together, packs upon their backs, and wearing their comfortable, home-made sealskin shoes (rivlins) and carrying town shoes with them. The journey was too long to be done in one day, and an overnight stop was made at a cottage about halfway, where a sympathetic woman provided accommodation. To cut a few miles off the journey and to save going right round the arm of Weisdale Voe, a long inlet from the sea, they paid a penny and were rowed across. The journey was resumed on foot, and when Lerwick came in sight, they stopped at the roadside to put on their best shoes. In Lerwick they sought out the merchant, who worked on the barter system, exchanging tea and items such as tea-towels and handkerchiefs for their pack of knitwear. The Papa Stour women knew that this iniquitous system was unfair, a cotton handkerchief of little value for a pair of men's socks, but they also knew they had no redress. And there is little doubt they were shamelessly exploited.

There seems to have been a good deal of payment in kind; on the island itself this happened. Men who worked at the fishing were often paid in fish. The boat owners and factors took the fish of prime quality; the next best was to be dried, or salted, for sale. And the workers got what was left in lieu of money.

The same sort of thing obtained when the Meal Road was built. This short track was constructed by the local men, who were paid a pound of meal a day for their labours, hence the name 'Meal Road'.

Today as I walk along it, or maybe look across the voe at the four tottering, rusty iron legs, which is all that remains of the once busy pier, or I step over the grass-grown hummocks of the fishermen's booths, I think of all the hands which built these things and all the feet which trod this road. And I recall the family names which have vanished from the isle—the Foubisters of Da Scaap, the Hughsons from Hamna Voe, the Coutts and the Twatts, Hendersons and Griegs, Johnstons, Georgesons and Sinclairs, and they live again in my mind as the wind soughs over the places where they laboured so long ago.

When men of the isle are in conversation together, the talk usually turns on topics of boats and things nautical. The older men, having spent all their working lives at sea, have a wide range of experiences to relate, and, as is the way of old folk, often relive the past with more verve and enthusiasm than the present. So it is from them that I heard stories of the wrecks that have taken place in the vicinity of Papa Stour; and they were retold so vividly and with such a wealth of detail that I could imagine they took place yesterday.

The earliest wreck in living memory was that of the *Nor*, a Norwegian sailing ship, with a cargo of timber, which came to grief on the Ve Skerries in 1892. No one saw the actual wrecking, but the first intimation of the disaster was the enormous quantities of wood washed up around the shores of Papa Stour, and on the mainland opposite. When the storm abated, and the sea died down sufficiently to allow boats to put out to investigate, nothing was found but the *Nor*'s anchor and the cable, so it was presumed that all hands were lost.

Undoubtedly the most tragic was the wreck of the Aberdeen trawler, the *Ben Doran*. This happened in March 1930, again on the treacherous Ve Skerries. During a stormy night the vessel ran aground, and throughout the night the weather worsened and the seas rose. Although other vessels were in the vicinity, there was little they could do. A Shetland fishing boat from Burra Isle called at Papa Stour to take a Papa man to pilot them through the dangerous seas. The man was John Henderson, our Johnny's grandfather. The great tragedy of this wreck lay in the fact that those who had gone to help were so near, yet could effect no rescue. Although they could see some of the men clinging to the wrecked trawler's mast, they could not get near enough to take them off. During the night the *Ben Doran* slipped from the reef and sank with all hands.

In World War II there was a wreck, but not, this time, on the Ve Skerries. This, strangely enough, happened on the eastward and sheltered side of Papa Stour, and was not the result of bad weather, but rather of misfortune. The vessel, the *Highcliffe*, laden with iron-ore, was on its way from Norway by the north-about route to a port on the Scottish mainland. People tell me it was the last boat to leave Narvik before that port fell into enemy hands. The ship ran aground on Forwick Holm, just below Willie o' Eastoon's house. Fortunately no lives were lost, and the crew were able to row ashore, but the vessel was a complete write-off.

These wrecks, having happened so long before our time here, have no real personal significance for us, but have in some measure begun to assume the qualities of old men's tales told round the fire.

However, in 1967, there was a wreck which could be considered much more personal, because the Papa Stour folk were concerned in it, or at least were concerned in the rescue attempts. In the early hours of Sunday morning, February 19th, a clear, calm morning, the alarm was raised, and the Papa Stour folk turned out to a man; Johnny, with the breeches buoy, rockets and life-saving equipment loaded up on his trailer, drove through broken and boulder strewn country over to the far side of the island to where the *Juniper*, an Aberdeen trawler, had run aground. The place where she lay was at the north-west corner, at a point called the South Horn, in as awkward a position to reach as was possible. At the bottom of a two-hundred foot vertical cliff she lay, and the angle was so steep that the islesmen soon realised that the breeches buoy could not be used. The nearest lifeboat, at Aith on the mainland of Shetland, turned out and took the crew off safely. No lives were lost, but it was found to be impossible to salvage the trawler, as no approach could be made from the landward side, and the shallowness of the water, and the many surrounding underwater reefs, made the approach of any salvage vessel or towing vessel impossible. To make matters worse, the weather deteriorated quickly. A south-west gale sprang up, and, within twenty-four hours, the seas were breaking over the wreck. From what we had seen on the Sunday morning, a complete change took place. During the subsequent days of that week the trawler, instead of being bows on to the coast, was turned completely round, first bows to the north, then bows to the south. We saw seas carrying away deck fittings and the ship's boat, and breaking open the fish holds. And each day at school, Gordon recorded in his diary the rapid disintegration he had observed, adding, with boyish humour, the comment that the seagulls were too full fed to fly. In no time at all, the *Juniper*, continually lifted and dropped by fierce seas, was broken into three parts and disappeared completely. And this, to my mind, was a most potent object-lesson in the destructive power of the sea.

These stories, and others like that of the Press Gang Caves, and like that of the wreck below the watch hut hill, of which there are no written records; these and others are of the sea. But Papa Stour has also a very intriguing story of happenings on land, and this must surely rank as one of the strangest stories of imprisonment and escape; for this we must go back to the early years of the nineteenth century.

A young Englishman of noble family, by the name of Edwin Lindsay, having refused to fight a duel and thereby held to have brought disgrace on his family, as a punishment was given a sealed letter by his father to deliver to Gideon Henderson, factor on Papa Stour. The young man was unaware of the contents of the letter, which instructed Henderson to hold Lindsay prisoner, as he was insane. At that time the factor represented authority and was all-powerful, and held the fate of the islanders in his hands, having sway over their lives and work, the houses and the boats. His word was law. Thus, no one on the island was in a position to oppose him. Henderson held Lindsay prisoner, accommodating him in his own house. I suppose this was a sort of open prison, in that Lindsay was not confined to the house, but escape from the island was impossible. No Papa Stour man would have been fool-hardy enough to help him get away, as it was noised abroad by Henderson that Lindsay was insane. This state of affairs lasted for twenty-five years, during which time Lindsay made several attempts to swim across the Sound, but despite the fact that he was a strong swimmer, the tides were stronger, and he was never able to make the crossing.

Then, by chance, in 1831, a Quakeress, Catherine Watson, came to the isle in the course of her travels. She met Edwin Lindsay and became vastly interested in his story, and formed the opinion that he was not insane. On her return to England she told Lindsay's story to several people, but nobody seemed to be particularly interested until a certain Captain George Pilkington decided to investigate it. In 1835 Pilkington travelled to Shetland as a preacher, came to Papa Stour and formed the same conclusion that Catherine Watson had done, convinced of Lindsay's sanity. Pilkington contrived Lindsay's escape, a very difficult manœuvre, as no Papa Stour boat could be used, for obvious reasons. So, leaving the isle and proceeding to the little township of Walls, on the west side of the mainland (an area outside the jurisdiction of Henderson), he hired a boat and crew, and, sailing and rowing to Papa Stour, picked up Lindsay and returned to Walls.

As soon as Henderson discovered his prisoner gone, he took boat to Sandness, hired horses there and rode overland to Walls, where a short skirmish took place, resulting in the contending parties appearing in the Lerwick court-house, where judgment was finally given. Lindsay was declared sane, and consequently freed; and he returned to England with Pilkington. There seems to be no record of any judgment made against Henderson as a result of his participation.

There still remain on the island a few links with that curious story of the Prisoner of Papa Stour. The factor's house still stands, though slightly altered. One of the wells is known as Lindsay's well, and although the name of Henderson has gone from the island, there still are descendants of that factor, but on the distaff side.

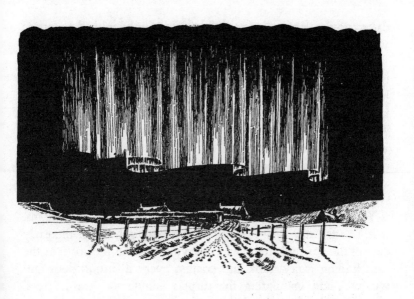

12 Winter into Spring

SOMETIMES WHEN I am in conversation with the older folk on
Papa Stour, and there is any mention of dates, I find myself in
rather deep water. The confusion arises because, way back in 1752,
when the calendar was reformed and Britain adopted the new
style Gregorian calendar, Papa Stour still clung to the unreformed
one, the 'Julian old-style'. So, if I chance to remark that the month
has begun well, in the matter of weather, I am gently reminded
that the month has not begun at all, according to the 'old style'.
There are twelve days' difference between the two calendars, and
thus New Year's Day is celebrated on January 1st, while Old New
Year's Day falls on January 13th.

When I explained this arrangement of dates to the children in
the school, and talked about Christmas Old Style (January 6th)
and Christmas New Style (December 25th), I fancy that they were
hoping there would be two of everything—two Hallowe'ens,
two Christmases, two birthdays. But I had to disappoint them. It
is in fact only the very old people who still regard these 'Julian'

dates; younger people, for their obvious links with the outside world, use the modern style.

With both old and new style calendars in mind, there is an interesting little observation which almost everyone looks for on January 13th, the old style New Year's Day, when it is a well-known fact that the day is light for an hour and a half longer. This, during the dark winter, is a very cheering thought, the first visible sign that the year has turned, and we are on the long protracted journey back to lighter days. I always picture this hour and a half of daylight as the first point to plot in the long slow sweeping curve of the graph of the passing seasons.

Yet there is an old saying which sobers any undue enthusiasm. It is, 'As the days lengthen, the storms strengthen'. In the early days of the year, when the wind is laying on from the north or the east, finding every nook and cranny, every ill-fitting door and window, and undulating the carpets despite the 'trassle trees' (those wooden bars fitted across the bottoms of the doorways), then it is possible to believe in the fact that Papa Stour is on the same line of latitude as Cape Farewell in Greenland, and as Bergen in Norway, and as Oslo and Leningrad. It feels like line 60°N even more when I go out of doors and try to cross the little yard or go round the school building. In rough windy weather, indoors seems almost as cold as out of doors. The wind, in gusty draughts, takes most of the fire's heat up the chimney. Our resident seagull, for all his cold appearance, grey and white plumage against a grey and white world, may have a chilly look, but I often think that, as he sits on the chimney, he must be the only warm creature.

The weather, in all its multiplicity of moods, plays an enormous part in all our activities, but the biggest single factor is the wind. This is true throughout the year, but especially so in the early months, when it can be unbelievably savage. The effect of its scouring action has to be seen to be believed, and it is no exaggeration to say that it removed the paint from the stern of our boat, and from the window frames, gates and doors, as efficiently as sandpaper. In our early years here, we did not appreciate its persistence and force. But a very strong wind, blowing steadily for about three weeks in the same direction, scoured away the dry earth which surrounded a rhubarb plant we hoped to grow, until at last, having eroded all the soil from around the roots, it blew the plant itself away, and we found it battered, against the school dyke.

The beach below the house, South Sands, is a sandy one, but in that same long spell of windy weather, the sand was blown off the beach, and funnelled up over the grass as far as the Manse Burn, a distance of approximately three hundred yards. The beach was completely denuded, leaving only its boulders and foundational clay, until subsequent tides brought in more sand.

The rough weather falls into certain patterns, and through the generations people have observed the regularity of these windy spells. The Equinoctials are, of course, well known; but, apart from these, there are periods when winds are rough and strong, almost violent, and these are known as Rees. What with the Pace Ree, near Easter, the Borrowing Days, and the Beltane Ree, at the beginning of May, we are often inclined to think that it is one long Ree.

A fierce wind makes living and moving about on dry land difficult enough, but when the Westerlies have been blowing at gale force for a few days, they stir up the Atlantic. Then there is a kind of delayed action effect. A day or so later, the rough seas hit Papa Stour. I have only to stand at the back door for a moment to hear a noise like an express train thundering away. This is the sea on the west side of the island, and this sound may rumble on for days. There are one or two places round the coast where the rock formation is such that a subterranean tunnel with a blow hole has been formed. In high winds and rough seas, the water is forced in so strongly, under enormous pressure, that a jet of water a hundred-odd feet high is flung out in a great spout. The first time I ever saw one, I thought my eyes were playing me tricks. I happened to be in the kitchen at the time, working at the sink, when casually glancing up, I saw a huge fountain effect beyond Jimmy Bruce's house. I blinked and looked again, and the jet came, high and unmistakable, and regularly. As Jimmy's house is on a ridge of land, and higher than ours, and the 'spout' was visible above his roof and about a mile distant, it gives some idea of the magnitude of the 'Spootie Hole'.

There is another Spootie Hole on the west side of Papa Stour, near Kirstane's Hole, which is more approachable, but no less impressive, and the force and the boom, like subterranean thunder, make man and his puny works seem very insignificant. I often think when I hear of funny little men shouting about Black Power, Red Power, Student Power and Trade Union power, I would like them all to come and stand on this cliff and get an insight into real power.

The Ve Skerries, that death trap of the northern shipping, lie about three miles to the north-west of Papa Stour, and are marked by an anchored light and bell buoy. But there does not seem to be an anchoring system yet devised by man strong enough to withstand the power of nature for long. While we have been living here, the buoy has been washed away, or out of action several times. On one occasion, on a rough February day, my husband out for a walk, heard a melancholy tolling, and following it to its source, discovered the Ve Skerries buoy washed up in Cullivoe. The buoy was smashed up, but its bell was still ringing.

It is no uncommon sight to see on any walk, at this time of the year, several signs of damage; a little fall of rock here, an ominous cracking in a cliff face, a new raw scar, erosion by the sea.

But it is not all destruction. There is a brighter side to the sea's roughness. The comparative calm after a gale is the time when we can gather one of the 'harvests' of the sea; that is, driftwood. As timber is not indigenous to the island in the shape of trees or bushes, driftwood is very important, and the sea is our only source of supply. After a gale, you can be sure of seeing little figures on the distant skyline, making their way to the strategic spots where a current sets in. And some time later, the same figures will return burdened with barrel staves and planks.

We soon fell in with island ways, in the matter of driftwood gathering, but found that there was much more to it than just walking along a shore picking up pieces of wood. It is an art, which unfortunately was never on any college curriculum. First it is important to know the airt of the wind, the tides and the set of various currents. Quite by chance I discovered a current marker from the Fisheries Research Laboratory, released from a point seventeen miles east of Wick. It had drifted to a small beach on the western side of Papa Stour. Gordon, one of the schoolboys, found similar current markers released from the Newfoundland Fisheries Authority, and these had washed up in the self-same place. It gave me an idea that this would be a good place for driftwood in the future.

Periodically we have a driftwood foray, taking a piece of rope to tie up any large 'finds' and an old rucksack for smaller pieces. There have been trips from which we have returned with very little, not enough to make lolly sticks, but usually we are lucky enough to find plenty to last us for kindling fires for a while. One of the tricks of the trade is to leave the wet wood to dry out, when it will be very much lighter, and easier to carry home.

One bleak Saturday afternoon, in the early part of the year, we set off for a walk in the hopes of getting driftwood, and headed for Sholmack, into which small bay a fairly strong current sets. My husband, who says you need to develop 'driftwood eyes', spotted a heavy log about fifteen feet long, just off-shore. We waited, trying to devise some means of grappling it. The beach, steeply shelving and rather unstable because of its shingle was made more difficult to negotiate because of a thick bank of 'tangles' which previous gales had brought up. We worked all that afternoon, weighting a rope, and attempting to get it over the log, and hoping to haul it ashore. But some freak of current perversely held the log end on, and tantalisingly just out of reach. Try as we might, we could not make that log swing round, and we left, reluctantly, when the tide was on the turn and the light began to fail.

But all expeditions are not so fruitless. One day my husband returned from a walk round the shore with a sweeping brush, and another day with a croquet mallet. Once I found a bundle of candles, and though not strictly driftwood, yet very useful flotsam. There is an element of chance, I suppose, in this occupation of driftwood collecting, as sometimes a place that would normally give a good 'yield' may be swept bare, and unlikely beaches well littered. Tantalisingly though, some of the beaches with plenty of driftwood are often difficult of access. Eckers Geo in the north-west corner of Papa Stour is one such. To look down from the cliff above, one can see logs and planks in plenty, but it is an extremely difficult place to climb, with steep sides and poor footholds. I did go down once, but only once. The descent was wet, slippery, and the surface was loose. But the ascent, laden, necessitated such an enormous output of physical effort that by the time the top was reached, I had hardly enough energy to face the two-mile walk home over rough country. And oh! how my shoulders rose, when I finally dropped my heavy load at the wood shed.

Really there was no need to carry the driftwood home straight away, as there is a mutual understanding that any pile above high water mark is someone's specific property and will not be disturbed. And in this small community, this rule, like others, is honoured.

So I suppose it would be fair to say that driftwood is one of the good results of windy weather. The wind does have its uses, and on a gentler day it is pleasant to smell the pungent tang of heather fires on the mainland, blowing over on the lighter airs, or on Up-Helly-Aa night to smell the woodsmoke as the galley burns in Lerwick, twenty-odd miles away. Jessie often says jokingly that we have nine months winter and three months bad weather, but, on the other hand, she does also quote the well-known saying that, 'Nae weather's ill when the wind is still'.

It is during this season of the year that the earth takes on that typical scoured look when the wind falls away. The grey rags of clouds cease flying madly across the sky and disappear beyond the mainland; the grasses, sere and brown, bent and beaten, lie flattened to the earth and show the grain and contours of the wind. The old crow that lands upon the school wall looks more ragged than ever, its ruffled plumage giving it an ungroomed battered look, and 'our' seagull which during the gales found it impossible to land within the enclosure now alights without difficulty and begins the eternal search for food. The relative calm brings out, from countless crevices in the stone dyke, starlings and sparrows.

Their survival throughout the rough weather is a constant source of amazement to me, as is that of the wren, which frequents some quite unlikely places in stone crübs and among the boulders by the edge of the voe. But sure enough, when the wind falls away, out they emerge, the Lord's little poultry, and what had been a desolate waste is now filled with busy pecking and darting to and fro. The pale wash of winter sunlight finds the blue-greens and purple sheen of the starlings' feathers, and reflects on the underside of the outstretched wings of the seagull as it glides overhead.

At this time of the year, we do occasionally have two or three consecutive days of calm, fine weather, a breathing space between gales, and on such an occasion it is a great relief to be able to get out of doors and to walk upright. Down by the shore, when the tide is low and the weak sun catches the exposed fronds of sea-weed, gently undulating with the movement of the swell, it makes it glint with a myriad lights. The motion and the millions of dancing sparkles hypnotise the eyes, and as you are drawn, and look and look, you can see this dazzling pattern long after, in the eye of memory.

February is often regarded as a colourless month. People picture grey skies, grey seas and no new life in the earth, but there is colour to be seen in plenty. There are rusty browns and copper of the dried-up seaweed lying in curving arcs in every bay, the bright green of the sea-lettuce, and the crimson, fine-branching, feathery weed that is often cast up on the shore; and the pebbles themselves, greys and white, and reds of tuff and rhyolite, the basic rocks of the island. There are the dark blues of the mussel shells that lie scattered in the shingle, and the brown and white of the razor-shells, and countless small ones worn down to silver nacre.

Up from the loch of Sholmack a dozen or so swans take wing, and as they rise and circle flying overhead, with necks outstretched and strong, slow wingbeats, the colour of the sunlight, reflected from the water beneath them, momentarily gilds their wings.

On all the stone dykes, the grey-green lichens cling shaggy and ancient, while rings of ochre and orange pattern the old stones of the churchyard wall.

As the daylight drains away in the south-south-west, the colours fade in the creeping greyness of evening, and the dim northern twilight settles over all.

A momentary calm may mean that the wind is merely swinging round into another quarter. We may deceive ourselves into thinking that winter is giving way to spring. Yet its hold upon the earth is most tenacious. The next day may bring another fresh fall of snow, and against its whiteness a flock of little birds, sitting on a distant wire fence, will resemble notes in music. The water of the voe will be turned again to pewter and against its dull gleam, a few ponies, tails and manes flying in the wind, will make a small, patient procession to the lee of the nearest dyke.

The school nature walks are not confined to the summer, and on such a day much can be seen and learnt. Well shod and well clad against the weather, it is enjoyable too. Tracking, following the prints of pony, sheep, rabbit and dog, and seeing the tracks criss-cross, looking for the prints of webbed-footed birds, and noticing where they land and take off again, tracing the swish of the wing-tip marks in the snow prior to take-off, all make fascinating study. It was on such a walk that we had watched the snow clouds passing over, and letting fall their curtains of snow on Ronas Hill on the mainland. Then one shook out its snow upon us. For a few minutes we took shelter behind a stone dyke while the air was filled with lightly-whirling flakes, and familiar landmarks took on a strange look. The boys remarked that it was a pity that there were all sheepdogs on the island, and no St. Bernards! They fancied being rescued in the traditional manner.

We did see rescue work, however, but of a different sort as we came homewards. It began first by us noticing the fragrance of hay on the wintry air; and Helen, who had been busy carrying out bundles of it to feed her sheep, was leading home a ewe in need of attention.

That night brought a wonderful display of the northern lights, playing coldly upon the snowy ground, and the ponies I had seen earlier in the day, were standing, close-packed, head to tail, for warmth, in the lee of the school dyke.

After that, winter tightened its grip on the earth in a cruel frost, and although we tore another page off the calendar, ice still covered the pools, and part of the voe and the sea-edge by Fiski-taing were frozen over. On such a night, when the moon was at the full, the island had a magical look, but as the time wore on and the moon waned, the magic faded and the scene took on an air of melancholy, as though the light had gone for ever from the world.

But there are compensations, even in the darkest time. To see the kirk windows shining from within on a dark night, and to watch the glow-worms of distant torches converging, as people make their way there: these are things that give a lift to the heart, and things I count as joys of the winter.

There are times in the winter, when, with darkness like a palpable thing, or when seals, singing in the voe with an indescrib-able sadness, presage more storms and gales, or when cold bites to the very bone, and the blasts of wind are like Skrymir's, straight from Jötunheim, it seems as if the winter will never relax its steely grip.

There are times, too, when the persistence of the bad weather has that perpetual feeling, often encountered in dreams, a feeling of a thing going on and on for ever. In the Sound, every baa may be breaking, Neepa Baa, Matta Baa, Revera Baa and Midsome Baa, all a lather of white foam; yet a discerning eye may notice that the snow round the windows has taken on that translucent look, and is beginning to slip a little, away from the frames.

Or on a day of grey cloud, when the sky has been lowering and overcast, a small blue gap may appear—this was what Billy, one of the pupils, so aptly described as 'the eye o' heaven'.

Perhaps on the very day when one had been reflecting gloomily on the only three fine Sundays out of fifty-two, in the past year, one had failed to notice the snow shrinking, now clinging only to the shadow side of the dykes, and the outlines of the little rigs.

Breaking in upon these gloomy reflections, Gordon, coming into school one morning, drew my attention to the sun shining obliquely on the shoulder of Hillafielly, where numbers of little streamlets, formed from the melting snow, were glinting in the morning light, like shining snail trails. And Billy writing in his book, observed, 'Snow to the north, snow to the south, but daisies on Papa'. It is then that one begins to notice the crevices in the dyke become alive with sparrows and starlings; soon the flick of a linnet will be seen, and the miracle of spring will have commenced.

13 Comings and Goings

WHEN AT LAST the long winter is over, and a gentler air stream blows in this direction, one day when it is possible to go out of doors without hunching up one's shoulders, holding on to one's hat whilst struggling to shut the outer door; that day, with its mildness, tempts bureaucracy out of its long winter sojourn in city offices. The hibernation behind the heavy mahogany desks is over. I can imagine all over the office world, clerks and inspectors, managers and officials, pushing back their chairs, stretching their cramped limbs and throwing down their pens, very much as Mole threw down his whitewash brush, and setting off into the great world of out-of-doors.

'Just the day for a trip to Papa Stour,' I can hear them say. And they set off, a steady stream of them.

They do not all arrive at once. A trickle comes for a start. Perhaps the Crofters' Commission men sniff the fresh air and set off first. Fences that have been blown down in the winter gales have to be examined, or land has to be measured before reseeding can be started. 'The very day for it,' they think, and they come, with tape-measures and sheaves of paper, theodolites and striped sighting posts, all ready for action.

Then, news gets around. On the next boat comes the old packie-woman with her enormous bundle of table linen and household goods, ready to do business, and bargain with the timid housewives. Then the clerk of works comes to estimate the gale damage and to note the necessary repairs to the school and schoolhouse. Not long after, come the builder and his band of merry men. The local music organiser may resume the theme of his lessons for the schoolchildren, a course begun on 'tape' the previous term, and interrupted by the winter. After his visit an inspector comes; the vet and the optician arrive, the minister and the social security man, the doctor and the coastguard.

It sometimes happens that officials meet at the same time at the Sandness jetty, and what strange boatloads that can make. The war graves commission man and the coastguard, the packie and the doctor, the pensions man and the school inspector, the optician with the clerk of works. This is all right up to a point. But some of them may wish to return at different times. The packie, anxious to dispose of all of her wares, intends to visit every house on the island, and requires a whole day for a sell-out, while the coastguard, a busy man with a full schedule of visits, may be very short of time. Once he has tested the breeches buoy and put the Papa Stour life-saving team through their drills, he wants to be away, to make similar calls at other places. But the Crofters' Commission men, meanwhile, may have met with unforeseen snags, and may need accommodation. So in this way the visitors are interesting, whether short term or long. But of course, all of them are at the mercy of the weather.

The milder spell may be a complete hoax, falsely luring them out from the warm comfort of their offices to the wilds. The wind may change suddenly, and then frantic telephone calls have to be made; accommodation has to be found and alternative arrangements made. Thus we frequently get strange bed-fellows.

Once we found ourselves with three Crofters' Commission men for a protracted stay. On another occasion, a lady bird-watcher got stranded. A lad arrived one day intending to pitch his tent and, in spite of local advice, 'live it rough', but he was the most ill-equipped camper I have ever seen, and, with tattered tent and soaked clothing, eventually sought the shelter of the schoolhouse. His visit coincided with the minister's. An ill-assorted pair!

Another ill-matched twosome, who actually came in each other's company, turned out to be complete strangers to one another. The locum vet, an elderly and very kindly-disposed gentleman, was one of the pair, and he, rather hard of hearing. It transpired he had seen a man walking along the mainland road and, very considerately, slowed down to offer him a lift. The man, however, was an ardent hiker and intent on a walking holiday in Shetland; he could not convey this idea above the sound of the car engine. So he eventually found himself at Sandness, at the end of the road; a trip to Papa Stour came without his asking. As I left the house to go next door for afternoon school, the bronzed hiker was eating his packed lunch in the dining-room, while the vet was in the kitchen, locked in an embrace with the dog, not unlike the last waltz.

On another occasion a G.P.O. linesman came for a 'one-night stand', and shortly after he was gone, my husband announced 'The gas man cometh', on his periodic inspection of the Calor gas installation. Spring in the air seems to stir all the officials into action, and remembering Papa Stour's existence, they sally forth.

The milder weather has its effect upon the islesfolk too. Like Chaucer's characters of so long ago, 'Whan that Aprille with his shoores sote', something stirs within the Papa Stour women and they too 'longen for to gan on pilgrimage'—not a pilgrimage in the strict sense of the word, rather an excursion. The womenfolk have a desire, and a need to get to the town, and to do very essential shopping. I occasionally feel this need myself. From September to April can be a long time. Things wear out; breakages occur; household goods need to be replaced; and although the merchants in Lerwick are most obliging, there are certain items of shopping which cannot really be ordered very satisfactorily by phone. So, along with a few other island women, I catch the spring fever too—an urge to go shopping.

As in everything else, this has to be a combined operation, and arrangements are always made with the proviso of 'weather permitting'. The day before the proposed trip, there is a good deal of telephoning within the isle, to check up on the weather prospects, the condition of the sea and the direction of the wind. For these things determine the whereabouts of John's boat and the point of embarkation. Setting off from the pier, if there is a low ebb, means that people have to negotiate the iron ladder down the side of the pier. Leaving from Hamna Voe on a low tide brings other problems, including a precarious clambering over slippery weed-covered rocks and a scramble up over the bows and on to the foredeck of the *Venture*. John always tries to bring the boat to the best point for everybody concerned, and, as always, is most obliging. He bears in mind the fact that several of the women will have been up since the crack of dawn, milking the cows and then preparing for the outing; so he brings the boat to a point which will necessitate the least walking for the ladies.

Wherever the embarkation takes place, it always means the wearing of rubber boots and some form of protective rainwear. This means that town shoes and other accessories have to be carried in bags. At Sandness, the Papa Stour people have a little shed and it is here that a transformation takes place; Wellington boots give place to light shoes, and drab raincoats are folded up. From under plastic rainhoods gay hats begin to blossom; and the party that emerges is almost unrecognisable from the one that went in.

Then everyone begins to glance along the road watching for the coming of the car. Thanks to the kindness of a Sandness acquaintance, my husband is able to have the use of a car for a day. There being no public transport, this is the only possible way the islesfolk can get to Lerwick. Hiring a taxi would be out of the question because of the high charges, making any outing an extremely expensive business.

A day's shopping in Lerwick is very much like the same thing anywhere else, except that in our case we are not buying supplies for a day nor a week. It may be months before another such outing is arranged, and the women have to think back and buy the many replacements, and look ahead and purchase the necessities. The little extras that are taken for granted by town dwellers assume the status of luxuries. After a long winter, when salt meat, salt fish, canned and dried goods pall, it is only to be expected that the palate clamours for a change. So it is not surprising that on the return journey the boot of the car, and the interior, and the knees of the passengers are piled high with boxes and packages of widely diverse contents. Out from the car and down the Sandness jetty go the returning party carrying their purchases. Some carry boxes of groceries; one has a saw with its blade wrapped in sacking. Several carry hardware, pails and bowls. Everybody works together, and it is a good instance of communal living to see cartons and goods so quickly carried from car to boat, irrespective of ownership. The important thing is to get them down to the boat. As the car is being returned to its owner, the ladies' gay hats disappear. Raincoats are unfolded, and rubber boots are put on for the return trip.

On one particular occasion, we put into Hamna Voe on our journey back. It happened that the tide was very low, and to get ashore necessitated a rather long and perilous scramble over weed-covered rocks—no easy business when burdened with a variety of boxes, bags and parcels. Lizzie's husband, Billy, standing on the rocks with a mooring rope, helped the women as they clambered over, and then in the growing darkness, cases and packages were passed from hand to hand, with warning cries of, 'Mind those cream cakes', 'Take care of this. There's a record inside' and 'Watch yon cups and saucers'. And as goods and people were coming safely ashore, a voice came up from the confusion, 'This is worse than the landings on D-Day.'

There have been much funnier embarkings and disembarkings. It is impossible to retain one's dignity while being carried ashore at South Sands, and it takes some visitors by surprise. Peals of laughter from the carried, and gasps and groans from the carrier, when one is asked to choose between a 'piggy-back' or a 'fireman's lift'.

A place which is used only very occasionally for a landing is Skibbie Geo, where the rocks form a very rough sort of stairway down to the water. We returned to this point one day after being at a regatta in Scalloway, on the mainland. But it had been one of those occasions when, combining business with pleasure, we returned home heavily laden. The ascent up Skibbie Geo was rather like an assault course, and gave rise to much laughter, when parcels, rather loosely wrapped, began to burst open and disgorge their contents. Wellington boots flopped out on to the rocks and new oilskin coats slithered out, leaving us holding nothing but brown paper and string in one hand, while the other hand held on to the rocks above.

An even trickier method of embarking was employed by my husband once, but this was from sheer necessity. It happened like this. John's big boat, the *Venture*, was in Hamna Voe, but owing to the state of the tide and the wind it was more convenient to moor in the shelter of the hill, where there is a gentle sandy beach. The water is very shallow here, and as the boat was lying bows on to the shore, it was necessary to wade out and climb aboard over the stem. As the *Venture* is high in the bows, John propped up a very long oar, wedged in the sand and resting on the gunnel. Up this he climbed, followed by my husband, like a monkey on a stick. Unfortunately when about halfway, the oar, loosened by vibration, spun round and deposited him in the water. However, he did clamber aboard and was none the worse for the wetting.

In all the many comings and goings, it is surprising how few real wettings there are. Our former minister, on a parochial visit, stepped out of the small boat, misjudging the depths, and arrived at the schoolhouse soaked from the knees downwards. The rest of the 'visiting' had to be done in borrowed trousers and boots. Perhaps the wettest departure on record was when the prospective Tory candidate left the isle. On the previous evening, during his miniature campaign, a phenomenally red and angry sunset lit up the schoolroom, and as the meeting disbanded, the topic of conversation was the coming weather, not politics. As people stood in little knots, many heads were wagging, and everyone was of the opinion that this fiery evening sky presaged bad weather. They were right. The following day it was as if the heavens opened. The sea was so rough that normally John would not have attempted a crossing. But as we had a guest who had to return to the mainland for urgent family reasons, and the politician had to return as well, John decided he would undertake the journey. We went with them, and never have I known such wild weather. Everyone was thoroughly soaked, and one of the most vivid recollections of the landing was seeing the politician remove his Wellington boots and literally pour the water out of them.

Some of the visitors who come seem to expect a fanfare. Telephone calls precede them, orders are given then countermanded, provisional arrangements made and as quickly unmade. This was the state of affairs in the isle before the visit of a bird-watcher from France. A frantic telephone call to ask if a certain fishing boat had arrived was made first, and I could picture the invisible Gallic gesticulations at the other end of the line. This call sent me running upstairs to put my head out of the skylight, a fairly good observation post. Then came a request for me to take a message to the skipper of the boat if it was at the pier; failing that, would I ring the caller back? Hardly had I returned, breathlessly, from the pier, when the phone rang again, with a mass of enquiries as to the weather, the state of the Sound and how to get here. And by the time many of the islanders had been taken from their jobs, had traced and retraced their steps, he arrived, composed, calm, and as neat and natty as any *maître de danse*.

By contrast, some people leave the isle so unobtrusively that their going is hardly noticed. One such was a camper who chose a quiet site on the west side of the dyke, at a place near the Loch of Ebbs and Flows. He came, he enjoyed the peace of the isle for a little time, troubled no one, then quietly departed, leaving no trace, except for one small brown ring, where once his fire had glowed in the dusk.

Because transport is so difficult here, whenever a boat goes across to Sandness, whether it is John's *Venture* or any of the other smaller boats, someone from the boat's crew always looks inside the Papa Stour shed to see if there are any goods waiting to be transported across to the isle. All the men are most obliging in this, and we see some very peculiar cargoes. Sacks of chicken food, bags of nitro-chalk, household goods, gas cylinders and all manner of things required for the house and croft are carried willingly by Papa Stour's little merchant fleet. One day, looking across the Sound, I saw a sight that appeared like one of Heath Robinson's wildest flights of fancy. A small boat, very low in the water, was laden with sacks of meal, several big cardboard cartons, a couple of bags of coal and on top of all this an inverted wheelbarrow.

Among the usual mixed merchandise unloaded at the pier were two long wooden forms. These were intended by George, who had made them on the mainland, as additional seating for any social occasion held in the schoolroom. It happened to be the October half-term at school, and we went to the pier to collect them. Some of the schoolboys had forestalled us, got there first and were carrying one bench along the road, stopping occasionally to sit down upon their burden. My husband and I carried the remaining one, and we must have looked like that famous Hall's Distemper pair, who used to stride along over so many miles of English countryside some years ago.

When the school's books and general stocks come, they, too, arrive in a mixed cargo, and maybe I am the only teacher who can lay claim to wheeling the year's supplies up to her school on a wheelbarrow.

The difficulty of transport does tend to make people use one journey for several purposes. It may be said to be combining several businesses with many pleasures. For example, if the boat is to cross the Sound for a school journey, there is always room for others who may want a trip to Lerwick for some reason of their own. To carry an extra passenger in no way interferes with the purpose of the journey, infringes no rules and obliges someone. I remember a school visit to Jarlshof, which was specially arranged to fit in with the history curriculum. We were bent on seeing this stone age settlement at the southern end of the mainland of Shetland. At that time it happened that Katie was a patient in Lerwick hospital, so the spare seat in the car was taken by Jessie who wished to visit her. The same transport which was organised for the pupils could serve two purposes.

There could be a great tendency in a small isolated island for the children to grow up with very circumscribed views. Long ago when the island had very little contact with the mainland, this was of no consequence, because everyone spent their childhood, grew up and lived their lives here without ever having to leave the island. Indeed, one old lady living on Papa Stour now has never left it in all her eighty-odd years. But with today's children, things are vastly different. All of them will eventually leave the island for further education. Rather than have each one take a very painful plunge into a much larger and slightly alien community, I have always included, over and above the normal school curriculum, visits and contacts which I feel will help to lessen the shock of impact when it does come.

To spend one's early years in a world approximately three miles by two, among thirty or so people, and to hear the voice of only one teacher could be a narrow world indeed. So whenever the opportunity has occurred, I have endeavoured to widen their horizons, with school correspondence, the exchange of 'tapes' and visits to places of interest.

And with that end in view, I encouraged the two boys to enter for the local musical festival. It was a source of great amusement to find there were so few categories in the prospectus under which we could enter. Not enough for a choir, nor a play, nor yet choral speaking; nor percussion either, there being no provision made for a one-man band. So, by a process of elimination, it whittled itself down to 'individual verse, Shetland dialect section'. Word perfect, but with considerable trepidation, we set off on the long journey. The day was a pleasant one, with sunlight on the lochans and voes, and new green appearing here and there. The journey was enjoyable, with plenty of chatter and questions, particularly at the sight of other traffic, and with just an occasional bout of nerves, when nine-year-old Billy bolstered up the courage of ten-year-old Gordon with such observations as, 'Man, man, it'll no be lang', and they fell to wondering what the adjudicator would be like.

There was only a smattering of children in the hall, with a teacher here and there, when we arrived, but the boys' quick eyes noticed that there were more folk in the first two rows than the entire population of Papa Stour. As bus loads of children began to arrive from outlying villages, the hall filled up. The boys' eyes grew round with wonder, 'A' yon bairns!' For an island child to see a crowd for the first time, it must be a bewildering experience.

But when the little bell rang on the adjudicator's desk and my pupils' names were called, it was I who felt concerned. To see a crowd was one thing, but to face it, quite another. I could feel for them, and see through their eyes that great sea of faces, palely glimmering in the darkened hall. Yet with that wonderful boyish resilience, they were able to get through their ordeal, and, returning to the anonymity of the audience, enjoy the efforts of the others. It was enlightening to me that on the way home, apart from their delight in winning, their talk was all about the size of the hall and its wonderful sloping floor. It was significant, too, that in the subsequent art lessons, crowds suddenly appeared in their drawings, as did traffic.

As might be imagined, the opportunity for educational trips does not occur as readily here as it does in the more populated and industrial areas. I often think back to the many and varied school journeys in which my pupils participated when I taught in England, for environmental studies, visits to places of industrial and historical interest, and visits of a vocational nature. Obviously this does not obtain here, but when an opportunity presents itself and has a direct bearing upon the lives of the community the chance must not be wasted. Such a chance came when an article in the Shetland newspaper announced the visit to Lerwick of a new large-type lifeboat. As all life on an island is governed to a large extent by the sea, and the men and boys of Papa Stour live and breathe and have their being in boats, a new lifeboat was of major interest.

The arrangements for the trip, and the journey itself, followed the usual pattern, but what a different atmosphere pervaded the car: suppressed excitement, speculation as to the lifeboat's speed and size, and all conversation laced with nautical terms. Upon arrival, nothing would do but that we made straight for the lifeboat's berth, and there Gordon and Billy ran her over with a professional eye, and stood back to admire her lines, like connoisseurs. However, the vessel was not due to be opened for inspection until the afternoon, and, not wishing to waste a moment, we made for the southern outskirts of Lerwick, to look round the remains of a Pictish broch, at Clickhimin. The school, at that time, consisted of three pupils—Gordon, Billy and a little girl, Sandra. At only five years of age, the passage of the centuries, of course, signified nothing to her, but it was comical to see her stocky little figure walking purposefully through a low stone entrance asking, 'Noo, where's a' yon Picts?'

Although all the children enjoyed this part of the visit, it was obvious that they could not get back to the lifeboat fast enough; and they were in the seventh heaven of delight when one of the crew invited us aboard. They saw every corner, every nut and bolt, ever rivet head. Radar, galley, engines, navigational aids, inflatable dinghy and its outboard engine; they saw it all. Unfortunately we had to head for home fairly early in the afternoon, so as to be able to make the crossing of Papa Sound before the early October darkness fell. But for this dismal fact, the school could have gone for a short sea trip.

We were fortunate enough during the time these boys were at school to be able to make a trip to attend a performance of the Children's Theatre, which was visiting Lerwick. This was the first 'live' theatre the children had seen, so different in its professional polish from the homespun of the island concerts, the only entertainment the children had experienced hitherto. After this I noticed the boys' activities had a very strong dramatic flavour.

But long after these trips are over, it is often the incidental things that recur in the memory: the sight, on our outward journey, of a heron standing by a peaty burn, and still there, and as motionless, in the greying twilight, when we returned; or fulmars gliding round the boat, stiff winged, planing and skimming the water; or the sight of that strange weather portent 'a gaar afore the sun', or 'a gaar ahint the sun', that arc of diffuse light before or behind the sun in its direction of travel, that signifies good or bad weather as the case may be; a bonxie or skua coming to rest on the surface of the sea not an oar's length away from the boat; or the startled flock of puffins, rising with a pattering of orangey red feet on the water before lifting up to become airborne with their characteristic quick wing-beat; or when returning round the south-west corner of Papa Stour, making for Hamna Voe, seeing the reflected light playing on the roofs of the caves in Shepherd's

Geo, giving it a lovely dappled look, as if lit by myriads of little lanterns. These are the little bright fragments that remain in the mind long afterwards.

As I turn over all these comings and goings in retrospect, I cannot help but compare these in my mind with the return journey from my last summer holiday.

I had the misfortune to travel from an outlying suburb on a commuter's train into London one morning to begin the long journey back to Papa Stour. It was full of men and women who obviously used that particular train daily as a means of getting to work. Nobody spoke. Everyone disappeared behind morning papers, or gazed, glassy-eyed and pale-faced, at the back of the paper facing them. On arrival at Liverpool Street, the train doors burst open to disgorge the human cargo, and each unit of that multitude disappeared down holes in the ground, en route for yet another train which would carry them on the next stage of their daily journey. Each one was wrapped up in his or her own affairs, oblivious to fellow-travellers, each self-absorbed, each a separate little unit, each uninvolved, detached, unaware.

For me, the end of that journey, after several trains, planes and taxis, was a rocking passage in the island boat, in company with two boatmen, Geordie, my husband, and a three-day-old calf. But, oh! the difference! There were handshakes, smiles and friendly enquiries. Everyone was solicitous of each other's welfare, anxious that the other fellow should not be wet with sea spray, and have plenty of room among the creels, and all most concerned for the welfare of the youngest passenger.

14 A Time of Great Activity

ONE OF THE peculiarities of island living seems to be that, for a very long time, life continues its even tenor undisturbed; then there seems to be a quiet and hidden gathering-together of events which bursts forth simultaneously, resulting in violent activity. This happens, in a small way, after a period of bad weather, when, after a monotony of grey stormy days, the weather clears, the sea goes down and the boat can cross to Sandness. There may be people waiting to leave the isle, others waiting to come in, luggage to be transported and an accumulation of mail and stores to be sorted. All this quickens the tempo. Figures carrying folded oilskins hurry to the boat; others follow with the luggage. And when the boat returns, it is as exciting as the relief of Ladysmith. A boat day is an event.

If this quickening of pace is apparent in a small way, it is equally so over the years. On looking back, it seems to me that the same must have happened on a much larger scale. Literally for years, time must have stood still, as it did for Mary Rose. Very little changed in the manner of living over many generations. Each spring the crofter dug his rig with the Shetland spade; each summer he made his laborious trips to Papa Little for peat; each autumn he cut his corn on the little rig with a scythe, and year-long carried all his burdens upon his back. His wife, meanwhile, carried her pails from the well, made her bannocks of home-ground bere meal, and in the gathering dusk, as the men returned from the boats, she lit her little colley lamp.

Then, comparatively recently, a minor rat-race caught us up. Some avant-garde isleman got a wheelbarrow, and that started it. Everybody wanted a wheelbarrow, and although the man's name was not Jones, everybody wanted to keep up with him.

Of course, over the years there have been small developments. Some of the boats got engines, and the oil lamp gave way to the pressure-type lamp, and eventually to bottled gas. But the real burst of innovations came more or less all in one year, 1963.

Never had there been such activity. It seemed that the 'powers that be' suddenly woke up and remembered our existence, and there was born 'The Water Scheme'. This was to supply fresh water, piped, to every house. Papa Stour is very fortunate in having plenty of fresh-water lochs, and the one chosen as a source of supply was Gorda Water. It is the largest, and the deepest. A very interesting geological fact emerged, that Gorda Water, at its deepest, is deeper than Papa Sound is at its shallowest point.

The scheme was quite an extensive one, necessitating the instal-lation of two diesel pumps to lift the water from the loch to a filter bed and reservoir on an eminence of land not too far from the houses. This was to give the water the necessary height, so that the delivery to each house could be by gravity. The digging of the trenches for the pipes interested the schoolboys vastly, and pro-vided much discussion material on the subject of soils, in the nature lesson. Of course, they were in the seventh heaven of delight watching the pneumatic drill work its way through the rocks.

I had my first drink of piped water at the Wirlie Hoose, amid much ceremony, with Martha and Mary. And, oh! how sweet was that first taste of fresh water after eighteen months of boiled insipid stuff.

And when the schoolhouse finally got its 'water laid on', there was no more fetching pails from the well. Nor was there any more working the semi-rotary hand-pump behind the front door. No more was it necessary to pump my way through every verse and chorus of 'Onward Christian Soldiers' as I filled the storage tanks.

1963 was also the year of the pier extensions. It was quite obvious that the original pier had been designed by a land-lubber, as it was dry at low tide. This meant that anyone wishing to load or unload any vessel could only use it at high tide. The short truncated design was most unlovely and not very efficient. In this year of great activity, the planners got busy and prepared to widen and extend the old pier and provide lobster ponds at the extremity. This extension brought the end of the pier into deeper water, and necessitated the employment of a diver in its construction. In no time at all, all my pupils suddenly changed their ambition in life. From trawler skipper, they turned their allegiance to helmets, weighted boots and air-pumps, and began seriously to consider the perils of the 'bends'. The boys must have spent all their out-of-school time watching the working at the pier, for it was amazing how knowledgeable they became. Their compositions were sprinkled with such words as 'caissons', 'concrete shuttering' and 'high pressure hoses'.

All this work necessitated a comparatively big labour force, and not having sufficient men on the island workmen from the mainland were brought in. As it was impractical to travel to and from Sandness every day, they brought with them a sectional wooden hut. This was erected near the pierhead to provide sleeping and feeding accommodation for the working week. All this injected a new bit of life into the island, and provided work for Mary o' Biggins as a cook.

When the extension work was finally completed it gave us a greatly improved pier, wide enough to get a vehicle down, and long enough to be used at all states of the tide.

But, as with the case of many of the official improvements in the remoter areas, it came too late. Though the islanders were delighted with these new amenities, they all agreed they were twenty years overdue. Already the drift of depopulation was under way.

In the early summer, another project was begun and completed in a comparatively short time. This was the replacement of the old watch hut by a new one. This small building on the summit of Hillafielly, looking out over the sea, is the place where the local men take six-hourly spells of duty during gales, to keep an eye open for ships in distress. The new watch hut, with its low protective stone wall and its wire hawsers holding it down to the ground, was well and solidly built, and supplied with telephone and signalling apparatus. The small mechanical digger used when the telephone cables were put underground fascinated the schoolchildren, and at intervals during the day, playtime and dinnertime, we noticed how far it had worked up and over the shoulder of the hill. Just as fascinated were they when the old watch hut came down. It was not demolished, but removed complete on the trailer behind Johnny's tractor, and, to the boys' great delight, at going-home time, they saw it inching its way down the hillside, looking at that distance like some cubist snail.

Papa Stour was not alone in all this flood of innovations; the island of Whalsay on the eastern side of Shetland was being supplied with mains electricity. This resulted in several diesel generating plants becoming redundant, and these were offered for sale. John o' Midsetter and his brother had a bright idea that one of these might be just the very thing for Papa Stour. They checked all the details and found that the generator in question would supply sufficient power to light three houses at the normal mains voltage. They asked us if we would like to join in their scheme as we were the nearest neighbour. Then things began to hum.

Negotiations for the purchase went through, and the generator left the island of Whalsay in the steamer *Earl of Zetland*, was unloaded at Lerwick, and carried by motor lorry across the mainland to Sandness. There the fun began. At Sandness there is no crane, so practically all the male population turned out to manhandle the heavy load off the lorry and on to the ground near the head of the pier. Then the problem arose of how to get it loaded into John's boat. The generating plant as a unit was so heavy and unwieldy that there was no other course but to dismantle it on the spot and carry it down piecemeal. I shall never forget seeing Johnny rolling one of the two mighty flywheels down the slippery jetty, and wondering if he would be able to stop it in time; each flywheel weighed two hundredweights. The generator itself was dragged down on a rough sled made of old fish-boxes—

a very ancient method of moving heavy objects, employed for a very modern thing.

One of the characteristics of Papa Stour people is that they get on with the job; and this enterprise was no exception. Once across the Sound, the separate parts were trans-shipped into Johnny's trailer and taken to the old byre behind the house which had originally been the Manse and was now the island shop. A concrete engine bed had already been prepared by John and his brother, and soon all the parts were assembled.

As the schoolhouse does not belong to us, but is the property of the Zetland Education Committee, we had to seek permission to install electricity, and, with the proviso that the wiring was done by a qualified electrician, permission was granted. The electrician came, as also did coils and coils of cable. Then a big dig began. The length of cable that my husband had to bury between the byre and the schoolhouse was comparatively short, being a mere forty or fifty yards, and the job presented no insurmountable difficulties. But for John it meant about two hundred and fifty yards to be dug, part of which ran through the swampy piece of ground which in wet weather forms an intermittent lochan known as Soutra Water. Everyone buckled to and got on with the work, despite the wet and cold. And one grey afternoon, just about tea-time, we heard history being made—the heavy thudding of the first ever electricity generating plant on Papa Stour. The electrician, a jovial fellow, chaffed my husband about his old-fashioned safety razor and invited him down to the byre for an electric shave. They returned smiling and pink, and smoothing their chins, with a very self-satisfied air.

The advent of electricity opened all sorts of new possibilities, and the ladies of the three houses spent much time in anticipatory pleasure, leafing through catalogues, and discussing the merits of electric blankets, washers, spin-driers and irons, and toying with the idea of television sets.

From the domestic angle all this was very thrilling, and, as we had the schoolroom wired at the same time, it opened up several possibilities there too. Much more convenient slide shows could be arranged, ciné was now not just a dream, and lighting the school on dark afternoons was by the simple process of pressing a switch, considerably easier than messing about with paraffin, methylated spirit and a Tilley lamp. Having electricity enabled us to light a little artificial Christmas tree for the children's pleasure, and when the time came for the annual Christmas concert, there was no end to the ingenious ideas for stage lighting and effects; 'floods' and 'limes' being made from old seven-pound jam tins. We had so many devices that Billy succinctly observed, 'We ha'e a' but the electric chair.'

Other islanders began to see the convenience of electricity, and, as in the case of wheelbarrows of long ago, this idea caught on, and other croft houses were wired, as well as outhouses and byres; and now there are five generating plants in operation.

Before very long, big cardboard crates arrived on the island, with 'FRAGILE' labels pasted on them. These were the first television sets. Everyone was agog to find out what sort of reception there would be. It proved to be very good. From certain points on the island, it is possible, on a clear day, and with the aid of binoculars, to see the television relay mast on the island of Bressay off the eastern side of the mainland of Shetland. Coming through a convenient gap in the intervening hills, the picture was sharp and clear, and the new sets worked well. The only fly in the ointment was, and still is, that only B.B.C. 1 is available, yet we still have to pay the full licence fee.

Television was a novel window on the world, not only for the adults, but for the pupils I taught. It interested me greatly to observe their reactions, especially when the boys ran eagerly to school in the mornings to tell me, 'I've really seen a train', or to voice their amazement at the size of a London crowd, or to express their delight in their first glimpse of a forest of trees. I had a shrewd idea, in those early days, that the boys were not always able to differentiate between a film on television and a 'live' picture. But this soon sorted itself out, and programmes of wild life and travel began to broaden their horizons.

Seeing the world through the television screen was one thing, but letting the rest of the world see us was quite another. It came about in this way. Two ladies came to see the island with ciné cameras and tripods and great quantities of photographic equipment. It was their wish, they said, to make a film of life on **Papa Stour** for television.

It was then the spring of the year, and rather bleak. The island had that bare, scoured look which is typical of March and April, when the effect of the long winter and the harsh wind is still evident. There was no new growth upon the earth, yet the two photographers found plenty of subjects to film. The unloading of hundreds of fencing stobs at the pier, the erecting of lines of new fences provided plenty of action, especially for the men with the heavy mallets. At that time the ploughing was just due to be started, and after catching the ponies and then harnessing them to the plough, John o' Midsetter must have walked miles while the scene was being filmed.

But the two ladies did not confine their activities to the land. They expressed a desire to film the west side of the isle, with the cliffs and the caves viewed from the sea. My husband and I were invited to go with them, and the trip in the *Venture* was one I shall never forget. The evening was one of those splendid golden ones, with the light playing upon the warm colour of the rocks of the cliffs and dappling the waters with gold. The westering sun enhanced the ochres and orange of the lichens that patterned the rocks, and caught the sheen on the plumage of the cormorants that rested upon them. With sea birds on all the rock ledges in such profusion and such variety, I felt I needed eyes all round my head, and I marvelled how the two film makers decided what to take for their close-up shots. There was simply everything. Guillemots in hundreds in rows upon the rocks, looking just like little old men in evening dress; fulmars gliding stiff-winged round the boat; kittiwakes and cormorants flexing and unflexing their wings; excited groups of puffins scuttering across the water.

At the entrance to one of the caves, Johnny launched the dinghy, and took off one of the photographers who wished to get some shots with a particular light effect. As Johnny pulled away, it put me in mind of Ratty and Mole who loved 'simply messing about in boats'.

In Muckle Huns Geo we had the sight of the evening. As the

boat engine was switched off, and cameras were being reloaded with fresh film, we were treated to a most fascinating aquatic display by the seals. So close were they to the gently rocking boat, that we could see, through the clear water, their every movement. Rolling and turning with consummate ease and grace, with their babies getting pick-a-backs on their mothers, they approached so closely that we could see the details of whisker, nose and soft liquid eye.

On returning to the house, it was generally agreed that Papa Stour was a photographer's paradise. Much still remained to be filmed, and the ladies planned to come again, saying, as they shook hands with us, 'We'll be back. Don't change the beds.'

They did come back too, but this time it was to record the Papa Stour sword dance in film. So the men, who had starred in such rôles as ploughmen, fence-makers and boatmen, now had the rôle of 'saints'. The filming of the sword dance presented quite a lot of difficulties. The men began to dance in the school, but there was not sufficient space to allow the camera to do justice to the varied figures of the dance. So there was no alternative but to perform it outside.

The only piece of ground sufficiently level was at the back of the school wall, but as this also happens to be a favourite sheltering place for ponies and sheep, someone had first to clear the ground with a brush. Then the dancers began to form up. One of the film-makers, with an idea of getting some variety of angle, suggested that a shot looking down on the dance might be worth trying. Everyone halted while she was legged up on to the roof of the school coalhouse, and, at a signal from her, the stationary figures became animated again. A nasty cold wind, blowing from the north-east, flapped and tugged at the men's shirt-sleeves and whipped their sashes about. And the little group of onlookers huddled closer together in the lee of the school wall.

When all the filming was finally completed and the ladies departed, the Papa Stour folk waited with great curiosity to see the results. As the weeks slipped by, and nothing appeared on the television screen, people began wondering what had happened to it, and there was much speculation as to its fate. Then news filtered through that it was to be shown in a magazine programme called 'Talk of the North'.

Each Friday, at the appointed time, all those people without television sets gathered in a house where one was available. Friday after Friday we went to our neighbour, Myra, and joined a little avid semicircle. Friday after Friday we were disappointed. We saw film after film of other places in the north of Scotland, and we fell to wondering if, as usual, Papa Stour had been over-looked.

However, in time, the Friday did come when we saw 'oorsels as ithers see us'. And there broke out from the little assembly cries of recognition as a 'weel kent' face flashed across the screen. The 'Talk of the North' became the talk of the island.

Shortly after this time, a visitor to the island was walking up the grassy slope past the Post Office; when he reached the schoolhouse door, he cocked an eye at the high aerial mast and remarked jovially, 'You do go in for big television masts on Papa Stour.' This was just his joke of course. The mast, a thirty-footer, is nothing to do with television at all, but carries the aerial for the radio-telephone link between our isle and the mainland. How far we have progressed, and how fast, can be judged by the fact that it is within living memory that the only method of signalling to the mainland was by putting a sheet or tablecloth on to the stone dyke, and hoping that this would attract the attention of some watcher in Sandness. Although the radio-telephone is a great innovation, ultra-modern and transistorised, it has its limitations, as only one message can be transmitted or received at a time. The benefits of the telephone in an isolated community are doubly appreciated during the dark winter months, and in gales and blizzards. Contact can be kept between people, a most vital thing in an ageing population. Once, during my husband's absence from the isle, and in a protracted spell of severe blizzard con-ditions, Katie rang me up daily, solicitous of my well-being, and before ringing off she laughingly said that we must sound, in our weather-enforced isolation, like trawlers, radioing each other.

About this time, not long after the film-making ladies had gone, conversation happened to turn on the way in which the outer world was fast encroaching upon us. Mentally ticking off all the new innovations, we found the list a surprisingly long one, water-taps, electric lights, telephone and television; and the list was still growing. It began to dawn upon us, that as new things came to the isle, old things would be discarded. We felt the time was ripe to record all the old things, before they were gone for ever. It was time, we decided, to make a film of our own.

I suppose, in a way, my husband and I could, in turn, be criti-cised for trying to keep up with the Joneses too. But this was not our intention. In our wanderings round the isle, and in our con-tacts with the people, we saw many interesting things of historic significance, old implements, and very ancient skills. So our filming began. There was no lack of material. I was especially keen to film Billy's grandmother working at her spinning-wheel, the last one in use on the isle. My husband was equally eager to photograph Gordon's grandfather threshing corn with a hand-flail in the ancient manner. Bit by bit, our ideas pieced themselves together, and rather than have isolated items and disconnected activities, we hit on a plan of filming the island throughout one year. We began with easy subjects, till we had acquired the art and probed the intricacies of editing and splicing. The editing device was home-made from a small piece of driftwood, two short lengths of copper tubing bent to the appropriate shape, a small section cut from an old aluminium teapot, and a bicycle lamp battery and bulb. And it worked very well, too.

Everyone on the island was most agreeable about being filmed. We explained that there was no need for special dressing up, no 'grooming for stardom' and no special posing; and we tried as far as possible not to disturb them while at work. At a rooing of sheep, for example, while everyone was getting on with his job, my husband moved around the group, taking shots, but not interrupting the work in hand. It was the same procedure with the ploughing, the harrowing, the planting and the harvesting, as also with the ladies at their knitting. With their willing co-operation, the film grew as the year moved on. Everyone asked about its progress, and when, at last, we had a showing, there was evident pleasure, and much hilarity, especially when, bearing in mind the previous night's sophisticated television programme of 'Miss World', from the anonymity of the darkness came the comment, *sotto voce*, 'Miss Out-of-this-World'.

Recording the old scenes on film led logically to the idea of recording the island sounds on tape. I am sharply conscious of the enormous weight of influence on the speech of the children by being subject to a Lancashire voice in school and a Yorkshire accent from the pulpit. If these sounded strange and foreign to the children, it made me realise that the polished accents of the radio and television announcers would be even more so. Being anxious to keep alive the Shetland speech of the children, and particularly the lilting Papa Stour intonation, I encouraged the boys to learn the local verse and to repeat it frequently. At regular intervals I included Shetland lessons, but often I found it difficult to reproduce some of the vowel sounds correctly, and occasionally forgot to pronounce the normally silent letter 'K' as in 'knee' and 'knock'. But the taping that followed was always greatly enjoyed; the poems, guddocks, the little plays and other original items in the local tradition gave the boys a good deal of interest and pleasure, and provided me with a whole new vocabulary.

15 Island Animals

BEFORE WE LEFT our previous home to come to Papa Stour, and were in the throes of packing, one of the removal men said (not so much as a question but more in the manner of thinking aloud), 'So you're going to live on a little island, eh?' Then surveying all the furniture, he added jovially, 'Don't you think with all this lot it might sink?' That was at the first tea-break. At the second he tried again. 'I did hear,' he commented slowly, 'I did hear on the radio about an island up that way somewhere' (this, with a thumb jerked in the region of his left ear) 'an island', he repeated with emphasis, 'that pushed up out of the sea, from nowhere, just nowhere.' He got his laugh.

Often since then I have thought about his words. Sometimes as I have been walking along the headlands, deserted and windswept, on some winter afternoon, with no living person in sight, I have pondered over Papa Stour's origin and its primeval things. What formless void was there before Creation sprang? What confluence of elements, what pressures and cataclysms, what upthrusts and strange mephitic alchemy to form such a place?

And after Creation, what then? What countless ages were there when rocks 'swilled with the wild and wasteful ocean' were slowly but inexorably eroded away, grain by minute grain, until caverns hollow and dark formed, and the sea's inrush broke off pillars like those of some immense cathedral. What slow, long centuries under sterile snow and ice? Then as the earth mellowed under the sun's beneficent rays, what grinding and gouging as the ice-cap slowly scraped its northerly retreat? Then after Creation, procreation of life. How, I often wonder, did the first moss spore find its way, to lodge in some crevice of the rock, where particles of soil and tiny drops of moisture made possible its growth. How did the lichens first start to pattern those ancient rocks with their ochres, greys and muted greens? And how, too, did the minute insect life arrive, settle and establish itself, the tiny midge, the flat pond beetle and the leggy grasshopper? By what strange quirk of nature are there mice here, mice—yet no rats, rabbits, yet no hares, and perhaps the strangest quirk of all, no frogs, toads or newts.

The island abounds in animal life—rabbits that honeycomb the little stack-steeds, where folk rested their loads of peat in times gone by; rabbits that nibble the tender green of the young kale plants and, emboldened, enter by the school gate; otters that come inland for fresh water; otters that leave their tobogganing marks in the snow; seals that bask upon the rocks, seals that sing in the voes. And the smaller creatures in their teeming numbers, and the quickly proliferating insect life under every stone and boulder, and in the hollows and crannies of a stone dyke. They always bring to my mind the line, 'Turn but a stone and start a wing'.

I discovered the wisdom of this in the high stone wall which surrounds the school area. At first I used to find this dyke an irksome thing. Grey, forbidding and dreary-looking in the extreme, it gave me a shut-in feeling, such as a prisoner might experience. It was most tantalising to reflect that beyond the horrid structure lay such loveliness. It was frustrating to know that spring green was appearing; yet not to be able to see it was a form of torture. To see fulmars skimming beyond it and disappearing behind it, so that it was no longer possible to follow their smooth circling flight, seemed such a waste of beauty. To hear lambs bleating and yet not see them because of this stony screen was at times unbearable. And occasionally, if the household chores could be left for a while, I would slip out through the kitchen door and take time to stand and stare.

Then I began to observe some interesting details. The ground outside the wall was considerably higher than the school ground it enclosed. There were many irregularities in the structure of the dyke itself, and these interstices afforded cover for hundreds of insects and many little birds; sparrows, starlings, linnets. Then, of course, the spaces also held a small but shifting population of mice.

So the wall, over the next few years, proved to be very fascinating and not the dreary thing I had at first supposed. One still summer day, a steady unhurried flight of wild bees left one particular cranny in it. Timed as regularly as an Air Force sortie, the bees emerged at intervals, each one zooming off on its course, no doubt to plunder the heavy heads of the clover bloom.

Perhaps the funniest living thing that ever passed the wall could be described as part optical illusion. There appeared one day, just before twilight, a shape that could only be described as a monster caterpillar, reddish brown and very hairy. It undulated its way along quite slowly, and proved to be, not a caterpillar at all, but the upper part of the back of Jessie's cow. The wall hid the rest of its body and its legs from view, and walking along the higher ground outside, it gave a rather horrifying impression of a gigantic creeping thing.

Cows on an island are a very necessary feature indeed, and are of paramount importance to ensure a steady supply of fresh milk, a vital factor in the diet. We must surely be among the very few people who get their milk really fresh and not messed about with preservatives and additives. To see Alex's cows knee deep in long, lush grass, or Jessie's placidly chewing the long summer day through, is only one part of the picture; the other is to carry home a can of milk, still warm, with its thick layer of rich cream.

From time to time on Papa Stour, there is great deliberation among the crofters over the respective merits of keeping cows, or keeping sheep. There seem to be two schools of thought. Some people bemoan the fact that because of the different manner of grazing, the isle was more beautiful when more cattle were kept and there were fewer sheep. Others, confirmed shepherds, realise the quality and hardihood of the Shetland sheep and the virtue of the wool, and base their choice upon this. The Shetland sheep are hardy, without a doubt. Born in May, as a rule, they come into a very cold world, with every inhospitable factor imaginable. Rain soaks them, taking away the body heat. Cold winds chill them, and because of the absence of trees and bushes, there is no shelter, other than the little stone dykes or the natural hollows in the ground. Predators in the shape of black-backed gulls and crows hover overhead, awaiting an opportunity to swoop. The paucity of grass for the ewes makes it a pretty poor prospect. They need to be hardy to survive.

Some indication of their amazing reserves of strength may often be observed in the winter, when, sheltering under an overhanging bank, the sheep become buried in snow. Some in the lee of a stone dyke become covered over by drifts, called here 'fans'. They are searched for by the men of the isle who poke long sticks down through the snow. It has happened in severe winters and in remote unlikely places that sheep have been buried for many days. Alex told me that one of his ewes was buried in a deep drift for three weeks, and given up for lost. But he found it, and though very weak, it did survive with careful treatment and good feeding. This must be the island's record for endurance.

Quite a number of Papa Stour men have a great reputation for skill with animals. Old Sandy is known to have set many a broken leg of a sheep or lamb when no vet was available; and on one occasion successfully stitched up a nasty gash on a sheep's side after it had fallen on the rocks in a geo. Lowery and Willie o' East Toon are also generally acknowledged to be 'almost as good as a vet'. This is a wonderful asset to an island to have a few pairs of capable and experienced hands to cope with sick animals. A situation may arise where it is not possible to bring the official vet across from the mainland. A cow may calve in the middle of the night; or a sheep, eating the seaweed along the shoreline, may slip and injure itself, yet because of the state of the weather, no boat could put off to Sandness. It is then that Willie or Alex will come to the rescue.

Just as the rooing of the sheep is a communal piece of work, so is the dipping of them, and in this skill a method is employed which is different from the method normally used in the south. A comparatively small water-tight container, perhaps part of an old boat, or in some cases a small concrete tank, is partly filled with the mixture of sheep-dip and water. Then each sheep is lifted in by the men and thoroughly dunked. After that, it is allowed to pass through the hurdle, where Katie keeps the tally. The men, Alex, John and Willie Drummond, hot in their oilskins, pause momentarily, while Mary o' Wirlie and Helen open the hurdle to let the next few sheep in; and the dipping continues.

The logical end of keeping sheep is market day, and here the great day of the year is that of the sheep sale. This is held on an open stretch of grass flanked by the churchyard wall. When the isle was more populous, this place would have been the centre of things, like an English village green. Here the pens are put up, and when the sale is in progress, there is often seen a row of little boys, sitting dangling their legs, enjoying their aerial view.

On the day of the sale, the dealers come across the Sound from the mainland. The prices at which the animals are sold seem extraordinarily low when one considers the price paid for a leg of mutton, or a joint of lamb in a butcher's shop. And when the animals have been sold, the crofters are often expected to keep them and feed them at their own expense, until transport can be arranged. This could be anything from one week to a month.

One of the things which is killing the islands is the very high rate charged for freightage. The charge for transporting sheep and cattle seems out of all proportion to the service rendered. Some few years ago, four cows were transported from Papa Stour to Walls on the mainland, a sea trip of about two hours, and in due course the crofters concerned received their bills. The total cost was £40, £10 per cow plus a fifteen shilling charge for clerical services, whatever they might be; and this for the County Council boat! When the crofters mentioned this to my husband, he was so incensed, he did a thing he had never done before. He wrote to the M.P. about it.

No island with sheep would be complete without sheepdogs. Like the human inhabitants of Papa Stour, who are mostly all related to each other, the dogs have their own intricate family relationships too. The family characteristic seems to be great friendliness.

The first dog I ever met, after our arrival here, was Gordon's. It literally threw itself down upon my feet with every intention of staying there. I had dismissed the school, and after the bairns had gone, I left the door open wide to allow fresh air to circulate. In came a black and white collie—Jip. I was sitting at my desk correcting the children's exercises and he padded in. Looking round for his master, and finding none, he attached himself to me. He crept under my desk and sat firmly on my feet. In due course, when my work was done and I intended to rise, he gave me a pleading look and held up a large paw to be shaken. When I left the school, he trotted obediently at my side, and I watched him make for Midsetter whence Gordon had gone.

Nell was friendly too; exuberantly so. We met her one day on the track, and she literally fell over herself to give us a welcome. Rolling over, she invited us to pat her and tickle her oxters. Johnny's dog, old Tyne, must have had a mechanical bent, for he would plod up and down every rig, following the tractor at ploughing time. The same friendliness that made Spot, at Braga-setter, rise from his place by the stove and press gently against a visitor's leg as he sat down, could be seen in other island dogs. Fan, Nell's daughter, at the Biggins, would wag herself into ecstasies on our arrival. Lassie and Judy, at the pier, would trot down to welcome the boat.

I suppose I had always been aware of the immense variety of living things in and around the island, but it was through the school and the National Nature Week that this became focused more sharply, The children's enthusiasm was encouraged by the arrival of the pamphlets, and we found our scope was almost unlimited. As one boy told how to fish for bait and described what happened on a lobster trip, giving fascinating details of all the unusual things found in the creels from time to time, others described the strange propensities of 'spoots' or razor fish; while some thrilled to bird-watching, others observed the ways of seals and otters.

We were able to record the sight of basking sharks off Kruger-setts, and a school of porpoises rolling and snorting and heading southward. While Peter, Geordie and my husband crossed the Sound and saw to their amazement a whale 'blow', we stood at the pier and saw below us a much lowlier form of life, countless myriads of small jellyfish, floating in the waters whence all life sprang.

16 Other Innovations

WITH ALL OUR modern progress and advanced technology it seems to me that man has lost more than he has gained.

Working in big communities, a complexity of living and a complicated organisation has reduced him to a mere cog. In the vast factories where mass production makes a man do the same repetitive job for the five days of every week of his fifty working years, he sees only that particular operation; his horizon is limited to a very small nut and bolt. And though he may be a most skilful worker, speedy and productive, yet, to my way of thinking, he is not a whole man, not free to practise many skills. He has become part of the machine, an automaton.

I often think of this and contrast it with the life of the average islesman, most of whom are able to turn their hands to practically any job that needs to be done.

Most of the islesmen have spent several years of their lives at sea on ocean-going ships. Not a few have been to the Antarctic and South Georgia with the whaling ships. They are men who have seen the world, and acquired a wealth of skills in the process. All of this stands them in good stead in the island way of life. And when they speak of their sea-faring, far from looking like the famous picture 'The boyhood of Raleigh', they do not just theorise about it, but put their acquired knowledge to practical use.

I bring to mind John's skill with boat engines, and the most professional wheelhouse which he built on the *Venture*. Many is the time I have been thankful for it; to stand in its shelter when the spray is flying and slashing across the windows, and to know I will reach the farther shore quite dry, is very comforting and reassuring.

They say that necessity is the mother of invention, but here it would be more accurate to say that necessity is the mother of improvisation. Papa Stour, like so many remote places, is suffering from a serious shortage of manpower. The boats which are known here as the 'small boats' really need six men to haul them up the beach and into the noost. Six men are just not always available. On many occasions, when a small boat has come into South Sands, the womenfolk have had to lend a hand. I recall the times when Willie o' Bragasetter's wife and Mary o' Wirlie, Helen, Jessie and I have been needed, either in the actual pulling up of the boat, or in keeping a supply of linns under the keel. Obviously all these people cannot be taken away from their daily work every time a boat has to be launched or hauled up; so ingenuity has to be used to implement the manpower. The only solution was to use a winch to haul the boat up.

The cost of a winch would have been rather high, so John o' Midsetter and Johnny devised an alternative means, dismantling an old lorry and removing the gearbox. A pulley was contrived, and was bolted on to one end, and a winding handle fixed at the other. The whole thing was mounted on a concrete foundation let into the end of the noost, making a very efficient winch. By this means, two men were able to do the work of six.

It is generally understood that in the remoter places, and in the rural districts, mechanisation has led to a labour surplus and consequent depopulation. But here, it is just the reverse. The numbers dropped first. The depopulation and consequent labour shortage have led to enforced mechanisation. Thus the few men left have to have mechanical aids. And these few men, in order to maintain a reasonable standard of life and to keep abreast of the work, must be men of many parts.

But it is not only in the work with the boats that the shortage of manpower has been felt seriously. In land work, particularly in the ploughing, sowing and harvesting, the scarcity of labour has been experienced. And with similar ingenuity, the difficulties have had to be overcome. Helpful as it is to have extra pairs of hands—those of relatives up on holiday—this is not really sufficient to solve an island's labour problems, partly because this 'casual labour' comes in the holiday time, which is not necessarily the time when the shortage is most felt.

It was this situation which brought about the acquisition, by Johnny, of a double-furrow plough, thereby shortening the time required for ploughing. After Johnny's work, the setting of the potatoes must be a communal effort. Up at the Wirlie Hoose, for example, apart from their own labour force of Geordie, Mary and Uncle Willie o' East Toon, there will be Jessie, Muriel and Helen by the time my husband and I go to join forces. And by co-operating in this way, the work which used to take a family unit about three weeks, now can be successfully accomplished in a matter of hours.

It may appear that the question of speed seems to be rather irrelevant, but this is not so, because the planting and growing and harvesting periods are so short, and work is very largely governed by somewhat unpredictable and unreliable weather. For instance, potatoes cannot be planted in a torrential rainstorm, nor can they be harvested in very wet conditions. So when the weather takes up, it really does mean that all available hands are needed.

The 'riping' or in-gathering of the potatoes used to be a time-consuming occupation when done by hand, but this problem has been met and overcome by the use of a potato spinner. Johnny draws it behind his tractor, and the same communal effort obtains in the actual gathering up of the potatoes that have been spun out by the machine.

The classical image of the reaper, the man with the scythe, working in the harvest field may look very nice and picturesque, but when, because of the labour shortage and possible bad weather, time becomes the all-important factor, the mechanical reaper is far more efficient. And here again, one man on the tractor, and another operating the reaper, can do the work of many in a fraction of the time.

Another innovation which, in its own way, helped to solve the manpower problem, but which has been superseded by the tractor, is a vehicle known as an iron horse. This strange machine consisted of a six horse-power, single cylinder, air-cooled, four-stroke petrol engine mounted on a small chassis and driving two road wheels through a gearbox and clutch. It had two long handles attached to the rear end where the controls were placed, and the operator walked along behind it, or, if it was attached to a trailer, the driver could sit on the trailer. There were, at one time, three such iron horses here, and very handy they must have been in their own way. But now they have been 'retired to green pastures'.

The transport problem within the island has been very largely solved by the coming of the tractor and trailer. But there still remains the old difficulty of transport across the Sound. This is particularly acute in the case of large bulky objects, and in the transport of animals. Any new large piece of farm equipment presents a problem. Formerly it had to be dismantled at Sandness jetty, brought across piecemeal in the small boat and then reassembled on Papa Stour. The reaper, for example, required several men crossing the Sound, working for some hours to reduce it to manageable proportions; then after ferrying it across piece by piece, they rebuilt it on this side. This was quite a lengthy operation. The same sort of thing had to be done for every unwieldy object.

But there are some things which cannot be dealt with in this way. For instance, no one would want the mammoth task of dismantling a tractor. It would be out of the question.

Then the same sort of problem used to arise in dealing with the transport of large animals. Over this vexed question of transport, the people on the island began putting their heads together. It was obvious, imperative, that some other means must be devised.

There emerged a plan to acquire a vessel big enough to carry a bulky cargo, which could be towed behind the *Venture*. The men of the isle had many meetings to discuss the merits of various kinds of vessels. In the end, a barge was decided on as being the most suited to meet all the requirements. This was to have a ramp to let down on a beach, to facilitate loading and unloading, rather in the same manner as a small landing craft of the Second World War.

Careful plans were drawn up, and the cost was estimated. Each household on the island made a substantial contribution; as the vessel was designed to benefit all in the community, all shared in the expense. To swell the funds, a sale of work was organised by the ladies, and many contributions were received from 'exiles' and friends. Then from a trust fund there came a loan, which was later repaid, and when the barge finally came to Papa Stour, there was great excitement.

Built in Orkney, it was brought to Papa Stour by the *Pole Star*, the Northern Lighthouses maintenance vessel. This was a very kind gesture, as charges for transport by the usual means would have been exorbitant. The *Pole Star* launched the barge in the sea off Housa Voe, and John o' Midsetter went out with the *Venture* and towed it into the voe.

Now when cattle have to be shipped from Papa Stour to Sandness, the beasts are walked down to the beach, the ramp of the barge is let down and the cattle are led aboard. The ramp is secured and the *Venture* tows them across to Sandness. There the reverse procedure takes place. As far as possible these journeys are arranged to coincide with the transporting of any heavy machinery that has to come into the isle.

If it is difficult to move goods and animals by sea, it is even more difficult to move people when they are ill. As Papa Stour has an ageing population, the uncomfortable question often arises of what would happen if any of the older folk were taken seriously ill and urgently needed hospital attention. Even if the weather is perfect, it means being carried on a stretcher over rough country to some embarkation point, and a half-hour boat journey, followed by a twenty-eight-mile ride in an ambulance to the hospital in Lerwick. If the weather is inclement, and the sea is too rough for the island boat to cross the Sound, the nearest lifeboat, from Aith, would be called out. The patient would be taken to some point on the mainland and thence to Lerwick by road.

These conditions do not only apply to the aged, but to anyone, in illness or in an accident, and needing hospital treatment. With no resident nurse and no resident doctor, some form of communication and transport at all times and under any conditions of weather is essential.

Each year, at the onset of winter, we hear many anxieties voiced. As the early darkness closes in, and the severe gales begin, the womenfolk of the isle, who have the care of the elderly very much at heart, become concerned for the well-being and general morale of those they look after. Many doubts and fears are expressed lest anyone coming into the island brings infection, influenza or colds. The people here are not normally exposed to these infections and therefore have very little resistance; and with those who are very old and frail, a severe cold or influenza could be most distressing, if not fatal. Often when I hear people say, 'We can manage, so long as the old folk keep well', I realise keenly what a forgotten people we are.

So it was with great relief that we heard the proposition from Captain Whitfield, of Loganair, regarding the construction of an airstrip on Papa Stour. This was to be an innovation indeed, and would fill a long-felt want. It was significant that on the day that he arranged to come to inspect the possible sites for an airstrip, the Sound was too rough for the boat to cross. This must have underlined the need for air-communication more than any words could have done.

He did arrive, however, the next day; and touring the island, selected, as the most likely place for an airstrip, a certain stretch of open ground to the west of Scattald Dyke. My husband called a meeting that night of all the islesmen. There was an immediate and enthusiastic response. Every able-bodied man volunteered to labour, and spontaneous offers of tools and equipment were made without hesitation. The very next day, Billy Tulloch on his tractor

166

passed the schoolhouse on his way to Scattald Dyke with a load of pickaxes, crowbars and wooden marker posts.

It was a chilly grey afternoon when I saw John o' Midsetter drive in the first stake as a marker post when the airstrip was first being measured out. The stretch of land to be prepared was five hundred yards long and seventy yards wide. Then the heavy labouring began. The land which was rough and boulder-strewn had to be cleared and levelled. The men worked for the next three weeks, prising stones and huge embedded boulders from their age-old places. The hollows that these left had to be filled solidly with barrow loads of small stones and gravel. The more stubborn rocks could only be removed by using a tractor and a wire hawser, while some boulders had to be split with sledge-hammers.

The men laboured on, giving every spare hour they could and working under very adverse weather conditions. Late November and early December brought bleak days and snow showers, and as the clearing work proceeded, the weather grew worse. It became bitterly cold, with a biting northerly wind that drove flurries of snow and hail in the men's faces. When I saw them still working, during those three weeks, they resembled nothing so much as a Siberian labour gang.

The women helped too, in their own specific way; Eileen, Johnny's wife, lent a willing hand with the stone-removing, as also did Lizzie, who meanwhile had been busy collecting white plastic bottles. These were placed on sticks stuck into the ground to mark out the length and boundaries of the airstrip.

After this colossal do-it-yourself effort, the aircraft landed. The first ever! Everyone who was able to do so came up to Scattald Dyke, and watched the plane eagerly as it flew in over Hamna Voe and circled round several times and then made a perfect landing on our own home-made airstrip. As I watched a Lerwick photographer take pictures of the men who had achieved this great feat, I reflected that this, to the islesmen, was just another job completed, and yet another example of their versatility.

I often think, when I hear the programme 'Desert Island Discs', that there are a great many people who admit to being completely useless on an island. Many of the people who are interviewed say that they would be unable to do the simplest things to support life; although specialists in their own sphere of activity they would be a sore burden on an island community of this sort where everyone needs to be versatile.

Whenever I hear these people admit their inability to fish, to build some sort of shelter, or to grow anything, I think of Johnny driving and maintaining his tractor with the care and precision of a perfectionist, and also of his skill with a knitting machine, and his energetic work on the rig. I think of John's knowledge of machinery and his practical hands, his care of the water pumps, and his quiet sympathy and understanding when he is the island's undertaker. I think of Billy Tulloch's massive land works, his roads and walls and draining schemes. I think of George who can fiddle non-stop for an evening's dancing, write a play, build a boat and turn a verse all with equal skill.

And of course this versatility is in all the islesmen, with variations. All can work with animals, understand good husbandry of the soil, can reroof a house if necessary, can handle a boat and make lobster creels.

In the women's work this is equally true; they are similarly versatile. A sock takes shape in Martha's hands, hands that not half an hour before were milking the cow or baking brunnies. Muriel can manage oars and fishing line with as great skill as with her knitting needles. And Lizzie's hands, which can capably deal with sheep's tethers, are delicate enough in their touch to create lovely gossamer cardigans.

Visitors to the isle occasionally use the phrase 'Jack of all trades'. This may be meant as a compliment to an amazing variety of skills in which both islesmen and women are proficient. But I never like to hear it. For with me it conjures up a picture of a rough and ready sort of workman who is satisfied with slipshod work; and this could never be applied to the work of the islesmen. When a man repairs his own boat, he knows he must do it thoroughly and secure every rivet. His life, and the life of other islanders, will depend upon it. When a man retimbers his own roof, he sees to it that it is firm; he does not intend that it should blow off in the first gale. A man with machinery, a tractor or a generator will execute his maintenance work with similar professional skill and care. A road will withstand the churning of tractor wheels, a tarred roof will be really watertight, and a dyke will be built to last.

17 Departures and Depopulation

WHEN, AS FREQUENTLY HAPPENS, the older folk on Papa Stour begin reminiscing of the years gone by, there is the inevitable mention of the sore topic of depopulation. To people who have seen every croft house occupied, every rig alive with busy people digging in the spring, it must be a most melancholy sight to see empty or half-ruined houses, and good arable land given over to sheep.

About a century ago, the population of Papa Stour was three hundred and fifty-one; and it was about that time that the drift away from the island really began. During the years when Papa Stour's population was at its peak, the rigs and the beaches would be busy with people. But this abundance of life was not only to be seen out of doors. It affected both the school and the kirk.

There are still to be found, in some houses on the island, photographs faded into a pale sepia, depicting rows and rows of knicker-bockered boys and pinafored girls. There were fifty-six of them in the school at one time, and the entries in the old school log book of 'overcrowding' and 'improvising the seating accommodation' sound like a cry from the heart from the school's one teacher.

A very different slant on Papa Stour's population bulge was

seen in the kirk, however. There seems to have been no complaint about the overcrowding in the pews—rather the reverse. When the pews were filled, the fisher-lads and men climbed the narrow stair and packed the little gallery. There are old people living on the island now who recall with nostalgia the lusty singing of the chorus-type hymns. The sudden drop in numbers during the ten years from 1871 to 1881 was due to the decline in the fisheries. Within a very short space of time, the herring stations closed, and the population began to dwindle. No doubt, as the teacher was recording in his copperplate handwriting, the school roll slowly but steadily shrinking, there would be, Sunday by Sunday in the kirk, more empty places in the pews; and here and there on the island, as evening fell, there would be another dark window and another smokeless chimney.

There was no alternative employment on the island, or on the mainland either. At that time Australia and New Zealand were beginning to offer opportunities and better prospects, so whole families decided to leave Papa Stour with the intention of building a new life overseas.

Some of these departures were not without their tragedies. One island family with several young children set off for New Zealand, but so long was the journey by sailing ship, and so ill found was their expedition, that some of the younger children died before reaching their destination.

From time to time there are more pleasant echoes of these early emigrations. The second generation of the emigrants occasionally return to the isle to see the ancestral home. There have been occasions when a number of these visitors have travelled together, calling their sentimental journey a Hame Faring. Even in the second generation, a journey to the island is still looked upon as coming home. There is something very moving in seeing these people visiting the houses where their grandparents were born, or walking along the beaches where their grandmothers played as children, or standing by a roofless ruin 'revolving many memories'.

I always marvel at the threads, tenuous yet enduring, which bind these folk to the land of their forebears and can pull them back from half a world away. So strong is the appeal of Papa Stour, that most of them wish to make a little part of the island their very own. Some take away with them small phials filled with sand from one of the beaches; others take fragments of stone from the ruins that were once their grandparents' crofthouse. Others spend the final moments of their visit taking a last farewell and a wistful look at the old ruin across the voe, seeing, in their mind's eye, the scene as it used to be—smoke rising from the chimney, and the small boat moving across the water.

Although the island has an undoubted hold on its people, harsh necessity caused the drift away to continue. The numbers dwindled past the turn of the century, and have continued to decline up to the present day. The educational system does little to help the problem of depopulation, by making it necessary for older pupils to go to the town schools for secondary education. This is tantamount to drawing away the life-blood of the island and leaving it impoverished. My first personal experience of this came very soon after I arrived here.

Already one of my pupils was due to leave the Papa Stour school and to go to the mainland for further education. This was young George Sinclair. Coming as I did in May, it seemed no time at all after settling in that the summer exams would be set, the marks would be added up, the prize day arranged; then the term would be over. As far as my pupil, George, and I were concerned, it was hello and goodbye within a few short weeks.

We saw him off, and as the boat pulled away I wondered what the future would hold in store for him. How would he like the big world outside? And what choice of a career would be his?

When the next term started with a school roll of seven, I missed George, with his ready smile and his meticulous books. Yet his going was in the general order of things. To the children, it seemed natural enough. The empty desk was pushed into a corner, and life went on very much as before.

But when the next departure took place, a very different spirit prevailed. Edwin, George's younger brother, was the next to go. The whole family had decided to leave the isle, and when the harvest was gathered in from the rigs, and the year's work on the croft all completed, they packed and sailed away. I had promised the remaining schoolchildren that we would hoist a tablecloth upon a pole, and wave goodbye to Edwin, as the little craft crossed the Sound. It was a November day, and although the youngest waved their handkerchiefs, and one of the older boys held up the pole in salute to the departing boat, all the children seemed dispirited. When at last they turned back to the school, their sense of deflation was plainly to be seen, in slumped shoulder and listless eye. Perhaps Edwin's departure in the middle of the term had something to do with it, or the dullness of the heavy November day; but deep down, underlying these things, was the knowledge that a whole family, not just one boy, had left the isle.

Very soon after this, another departure took place, and this one had the most far-reaching effects of them all. It did not only affect the school. I lost another two pupils, my only girls, and was left with an all-boys' school. But the kirk lost an elder, and its congregation was further depleted; then the shop and post office not only changed hands, but changed premises too. All this happened when Alex, the shopman, and his family left the isle.

At their going, Lowery and his family departed too, and as Lowery had been the postman, someone else had to be found to deliver the mail. Then it was that Mary o' Biggins became our first post-lady.

For some time after these departures there was little change on the island. The school roll stood at four. The even tenor of life continued for some little while, until Willie o' Bragasetter decided to move, with his family, to the mainland. This did not affect the school, yet their going left not only an empty house, but a vacant spot in our day. We missed Willie's cheery wave and greeting as he passed the house on his way to the shop.

As one year succeeded another, the sad subtraction sum went on. Michael first, then John after him, sat the eleven-plus examination and subsequently left the island to go to Lerwick school. My school roll was now reduced to two—namely, Gordon and Billy, except for two short spells when Sandra attended the school temporarily. But, as time went on, I was very often teaching a single pupil, as Billy became seriously ill. But a worse blow was yet to fall.

One morning, towards the end of the arithmetic lesson, there was a knock upon the school door, and Mary stood there with the post. For her to come to the school door was a most unusual thing indeed. Her normal practice was to deliver the mail at the schoolhouse. There was something so downcast and sad about her mien as she bent to take the letters from the bag that I felt a sudden premonition. She murmured an apology for interrupting school, and when she looked up her eyes were brimming with tears, and her face red from weeping. Billy had died, she said.

It is difficult to express the rush of feelings that overwhelmed me; grief, shock, pity for his parents, sympathy for Mary, his aunt, and an infinite sadness. What I said, I do not remember, but when she had gone, I stood for one brief moment in the cloakroom thinking of the first thing, the immediate thing, to be done.

Gordon sat in the quiet schoolroom, alone; the door had been left open; so it was most likely he would have heard our voices and already have learnt the sad news. In any case, he would guess it from my face. In less time than it took to re-enter the schoolroom, what I must say had already formed in my mind, 'Except a grain of wheat fall into the ground and die, it abideth alone.'

It was the voar, the time of planting. Corn and grains of wheat were something Gordon understood. We faced each other, each feeling a terrible loss. He had lost his only school friend, his companion of his leisure hours, his cousin. I had lost half my school; it was my private Aberfan. Keeping my voice as level and unemotional as I could, I tried to soften the blow, to stimulate his understanding, to explain, to comfort, to convince, 'except a grain of wheat . . .'

For the next few months Gordon was my only pupil. The school roll was down to one, and when the time came for him to go to Lerwick, the school closed. For the first time since it had been opened, there was no child of school age on the island.

That day, as Gordon gathered up his books and closed his desk, there was broken a link in the long island history. High up on the schoolroom wall was the photograph of the old bearded schoolmaster of eighty years ago. I reflected upon the gulf which lay between his times and mine. The room once so full of children now echoed hollowly as Gordon rose to go. And as he reached for his schoolbag and took his coat from the row of empty pegs and made his solitary way home, I stood at the door and looked back at the deserted room, sensing the poignancy of the moment.

There was a brief re-opening a year later when Eileen came of school age, and was enrolled as a pupil. But this lasted only two terms until her family, like others before them, left for the mainland.

Depopulation seems to affect the people who remain in two very different ways. For some people, the constant subtraction brings with it a feeling of desertion and abandonment. An air of being forgotten seems to hang over everything for a time, and while this depression persists, morale is at a low ebb. In some people, however, the departure of yet another family seems to bring out the 'soldiering on' attitude. They accept the extra duties and responsibilities with a willingness that is vital to the well-being of so small a community.

This co-operation was markedly manifest when, after the last family left, the rota of men on the bad weather watch was depleted and reduced to four. In spells of rough weather this necessitated Alex, John, Billy Tulloch and Willie Drummond each taking a watch of six hours' duration throughout the continuous gales. The fact of having only four men meant that the same period of watch fell to the same man. During one protracted gale, Willie Drummond passed the schoolhouse regularly at 11.45 p.m. on his way to the watch hut hill. As I lay luxuriating in the warmth of bed, while the storm raged outside and rain streamed down the skylight, I saw two flashes of light. Two flashes and then darkness. This was Willie's usual signal, and I spared him a thought as he battled his way to Hillafielly in the teeth of the gale. On that very night, astronauts in Apollo XII were speeding to the moon and busy sending back their wonderful television signals. But the double flash from a small torch was of more significance to us in our island context than the highly sophisticated radio signals from space.

If, after the departure of a family, a mood of depression settles over the island for a while, this is understandable. Another house stands empty, another window is darkened, another chimney smokeless, and there is another gap in the community. But, when the opposite happens, and someone decides to settle on the island, it gives a tremendous boost to morale. The effect is amazing.

This happened when Katie, Jessie's older sister, decided, in her retirement, to return to her native isle. The news was as good as a tonic. And even people who were not closely connected felt a lift of the spirit at the thought. It was not just the sight of a boat laden with furniture, coming to the island instead of leaving it, that gladdened everyone. Nor was it only the sight of a lit window and a smoking chimney; but rather the knowledge that someone was returning to the isle, that someone believed sufficiently in the future of the island to wish to settle here.

Just as Katie's return to Papa Stour and her subsequent settling in Hillydales gave a perceptible lift to the island, so did the arrival of a daughter for Johnny and Eileen. Born in the spring of the year, her coming brought with it a feeling of renewal; and knowing that there was now young life on the island, everyone felt a sense of continuity.

18 Time Marches On

ANYONE LIVING WITHIN sight and sound of the sea is in a marvellous position to understand what poets call mutability and change.

A severe gale and a heavy sea may wear away a familiar land-
mark. A strong wind-whipped tide may wash away much of the
sand from a beach, leaving all the boulders exposed. Incessant
scouring winds may blow away any sand that remains. So, to the
observant eye, changes may appear; a little fall of rock, a cliff
becoming more undercut with each successive winter, another
fence post washed away.

Yet, while this subtle subtraction is going on in one part of the
island, wind and weather may be doing just the opposite else-
where, piling up in another cove silt, sand and seaweed as never
before. And where once a rivulet ran out, mingling the fresh
water with the salt, a miniature Chesil Beach may arise. An ayre
may be begun, tide after tide adding stones and shingle.

These changes in the basic things of the island are elemental,
slow and imperceptible to the unobservant eye. More obvious,
however, are the changes in what might be termed the surface
of things.

When the sun's rays are approaching the horizontal and they fall, with lengthening shadows, across what was once cultivated land, my eye follows the contours of the old rigs, now grass grown. And although I repeople the scene in my mind's eye, with busy folk delling, Nature has already reclothed it in a covering of green.

The old long-disused noosts lying side by side, where once the boats were deeply secure, now are moss-grown, and seem little more than shallow green corrugations round the shores of the voes. The slow process of Nature's levelling, while filling the hollows, is, at the same time, reducing the remains of the stone walls of the fishermen's booths to mere green mounds, leaving only the hummocky outline of the site. Between the stones of the deserted paths, moss creeps and grasses grow, and the ways that were once busy and much frequented now no longer know the tread of feet but are quiet and forgotten.

The stone slabs which formed the rough bridges that once spanned the burns are awry, fallen or displaced. The narrow water channels to the mills, dug out so long ago and with so much labour, are choked with weed and débris and overgrown with mosses. The mills themselves are ruined, with their roofs gone and their walls falling in, and their stones, which will turn no more, slowly being covered by the encroaching green.

Sad as these sights may appear, there is no more melancholy a picture than that of a house long empty. The air of desertion hangs over its crumbling chimney, and silence over its threshold. While its outer walls stand and it is still recognisable as a house, it retains a certain amount of personality, and, in a sense, it is still inhabited. A fulmar may settle upon its gable end; a crow may alight upon its sagging lintel, a starling or blackbird may seek the crevices round its empty window. But as it reverts further, it loses even these shreds of personality and becomes a mere lifeless rectangle of stones, choked by thistle and docken, and soon to be received back into the earth.

Changes are to be seen almost everywhere out of doors. Ancient boundary walls, the purpose of which has long since been forgotten, fall away and become covered on the leeward side with shaggy grey-green lichen. The circle of stones enclosing the ancient burial ground of some unknown shipwrecked sailors is likewise overgrown, half sunken in the earth and mossed over. Dykes and dwellings, mills and paths, noosts and booths become weathered by the wind and by the inexorable passing of Time.

If the effect of Time can be seen out of doors, the changes that Time brings with it are even more noticeable from the human angle. I was made vividly aware of a sense of history and the passage of time when we were invited to the Diamond Wedding celebrations of our neighbours at Midsetter. The old couple, Jessie's parents, octogenarians both, sat there smiling contentedly and looking at the Queen's telegram. This, in itself, was history, being the first such telegram ever to be received on Papa Stour. As the flash-bulbs fixed the scene as a moment in time, it came to me suddenly that, here in this croft house, Time had unrolled a whole new changing pattern.

A casual observer might have thought that such modern photographic equipment was highly incongruous, yet this is indicative of the swiftness of change taking place here.

Dazed by all the bustle going on around them, the old lady would repeat, 'It's awful kind o' the Queen', while the old man said with wonder, 'It's come a' the way frae yon muckle hoose' (Buckingham Palace). These festivities, and the sixty years they celebrated, pinpointed sharply the swiftness of change on this island.

For generations, the way of life on Papa Stour hardly changed at all. For generations, the husbandry of the soil followed the same time-honoured pattern. For generations, the men of the isle observed the same customs, and the same superstitions, regarding fishing and the boats. The fathers passed on their knowledge of the sea and its ways, the weather and its vagaries, to the sons who followed after them. The womenfolk, similarly, initiated their daughters into the intricacies of the traditional patterns of knitting, patterns which had been carried in the mind over the years.

Through these many generations there developed a way of life that was unique. It had its own special rhythms, a time to dell, and a time to 'ripe', a time to roo and a time to spin. The winter with its long dark nights, and the brief summer with its long light days, succeeded each other in what must have seemed to these people an ordered and elemental rhythm. In the cold light of many a dawn the crofter wife would be tending her lambs, and in the warmer light of evening her man would still be fishing in the voe.

Although Nature's cycle remains the same, the affairs of man have suddenly changed enormously. The great acceleration in man's progress which typifies the last hundred and fifty years has manifested itself in Papa Stour well within one man's lifetime. Progress has come swiftly; and our neighbours, in their sixty years of married life, have seen all the changes.

The old man still recounts the long walk to Lerwick with his sea-chest upon his back, to sign on as ship's crew. The old lady remembers the same twenty-eight miles' walk in her home-made seal-skin rivlins; on her back, a bag of knitwear to be bartered for tea and other commodities.

And while he is reliving, in the manner of the old, the days of oars and sail, she will recall the cameraderie of the fisher-lassies in the days before the decline of the island herring fishery.

She has often told me how to prepare fish oil to fill a colley lamp, and how nervous she felt when she first encountered the complications of a paraffin lamp. Her fading eyes have run the whole gamut of artificial light, from fish oil, paraffin, to pressure lamps, bottled gas and now electricity.

He, as a crofter, has seen a parallel transition, but this in ways of carrying. His shoulders and hands bear ample witness to this; and from using clibbers upon a pony's back, he has passed on to the possession of a wheelbarrow, and now, a tractor and trailer.

Similarly, in this sudden burst of change, many of the croft-houses are rich in anachronisms; a hand-flail by the porch door, and an ultra-modern television set by the stove; an outhouse accommodating a modern diesel electric generating plant adjoining another where a hand-operated quern is housed.

No longer are seals caught for making rivlins; no longer do all the women spin their own wool. Instead the mail order catalogues have ousted the ancient skills. A weekly delivery of tasteless, town-baked bread has replaced the wholesome products of the island's corn rigs and water mills. No longer is practised the old art of telling the time by the sun. In place of watching significant shadows, like those on the kirk wall, the impersonal hands of the clock, or the artificial pips of the radio, now divide up the day.

It is a popular idea to indulge in sentimentality over islands, yearning for the old days and decrying all the modern advance. Yet the advent of amenities such as piped water, radio-telephone and home-generated electricity with all its labour-saving devices for the home, mechanisation of land work and engines in the boats, have saved this island as its population declined.

But, ironically enough, with the coming of these benefits, there has been a drift of the younger generation, some overseas and to centres of industry, in keeping with the general overall pattern of depopulation of the remoter areas. This is all bound up with the swiftly changing nature of things, changes in living conditions, changes in educational facilities, changes in thinking, and consequent upon this, changes in ambitions and hopes for the future.

So, while the younger generation of Papa Stour is scattered as far distant as New York and New Zealand, the old folks' world has shrunk to the confines of their croft house. In a subtle sense, they embrace the whole world through their family, and despite the teeming ideas and quick proliferation of thought which are beginning to beat upon the shore, my old neighbours can mull things over, sorting out the worthwhile from the dross, islanded in quiet.

Of all the many changes that Time has wrought, the one which had the most personal impact was the depopulation causing the final closure of the school. The lack of schoolchildren on the island impinged directly upon our lives, schoolchildren being my *raison d'être*. So it became apparent that a move was inevitable.

Our belongings were packed, awaiting the arrival of the *Spes Clara*, the converted fishing-boat which was to carry our furniture and goods away. And when the last crate was nailed down, and the tractors and trailers had departed, swaying with their heavy loads along the rough island road, we made our way over Da Murrens to the airstrip, reflecting ironically that the first and only occasion on which I was to use it was for a one-way trip. To offset this melancholy thought, there was a sight to cheer me. People were already emerging from the gates in the stone dyke and standing in little knots. Everyone who was able had left their work among the corn that August afternoon to come up and wish us God-speed. The warmth of their handclasps and the sincerity of their wishes made a tremendous send-off and helped me over a bad moment of departure. And when I heard the distant drone of the Islander aircraft, and finally climbed aboard, I noticed among the upturned faces the same two people who had helped us ashore that day in May so many years ago.

As the aircraft turned into the wind, became airborne and finally gathered height, the individual faces became blurred, and the waved handkerchiefs mere fluttering specks. The pilot made a wide sweeping curve over Hamna Voe and set his course southward. As the island fell astern, the familiar and well-loved contours receded into the hazy distances, until nothing was left but the wide expanse of the sea.

GLOSSARY

airt: direction from which the wind blows

ask: haze, mist

ayre: small beach

baas: sunken rocks

bewast: to the westward of

bowes: buoys

brunnies: small baked cakes

cairding: carding of wool

cappies: sinkers for fishing lines

clibbers: wooden pack saddle

cole: small hay stack

courtit: courted

creepie: stool

crüb: small stone enclosure

delling: digging

fann: snowdrift

geo: steep-sided inlet from the sea

grind: gate

gying: a row (*sweerie gying:* the first row)

haa: hall

hairst: harvest

hoidin: hiding

kent: known

kye: cows

kyettle: kettle

laachin: laughing

lum: chimney

luya: a variety of fish

maa: gull

medes: bearings

misforen knots: knots in a boat's planking supposed to be unlucky

moder-dy: movement in the sea by which fishermen could steer their boats to the land

moorit: a natural (undyed) brown shade of wool

oxters: armpits

peerie: little

rivlins: home made seal-skin shoes

ripe: to dig the potato crop

scoarie: young gull

scrime: make out or discern

shott: compartment of boat where fish are kept

shüns: small reedy lochs

simmer: summer

spoots: razor-fish

sweeing: stinging, smarting

taft: seat in a boat

tangles: thick stalks of seaweed

tattie rigs: potato rows

tilfers: boat floorboards

tirricks: Arctic terns

trokers: tourists, trippers

towes: fishing lines

unken: strange, unknown

voar: springtime
voe: bay, or open inlet from the sea
vooers: wooers

wa': wall
wilsom: liable to make one lose the way: misleading
yaird: enclosed garden